OECD Public Governance Reviews

Hungary: Public Administration and Public Service Development Strategy, 2014-2020

This work is published under the responsibility of the Secretary-General of the OECD. The opinions expressed and arguments employed herein do not necessarily reflect the official views of OECD member countries.

This document, as well as any data and any map included herein, are without prejudice to the status of or sovereignty over any territory, to the delimitation of international frontiers and boundaries and to the name of any territory, city or area.

Please cite this publication as:
OECD (2017), *Hungary: Public Administration and Public Service Development Strategy, 2014-2020*, OECD Public Governance Reviews, OECD Publishing, Paris.
http://dx.doi.org/10.1787/9789264286535-en

ISBN 978-92-64-28398-5 (print)
ISBN 978-92-64-28653-5 (PDF)

Series: OECD Public Governance Reviews
ISSN 2219-0406 (print)
ISSN 2219-0414 (online)

The statistical data for Israel are supplied by and under the responsibility of the relevant Israeli authorities. The use of such data by the OECD is without prejudice to the status of the Golan Heights, East Jerusalem and Israeli settlements in the West Bank under the terms of international law.

Photo credits: Cover © Bakhtiar Zein/Shutterstock.com

Foreword

This report is the final product of the OECD-Hungary Strategic Partnership project, which also includes the 2015 publications *Review of the Territorial State Administration of Hungary* and *Government at a Glance: How Hungary compares*. After presenting a brief overview of the results of the public sector reforms known as the "Magyary Programmes" carried out between 2010 and 2013, the report analyses Hungary's Public Administration and Public Service Development Strategy (PAPSDS) 2014-2020 and provides practical recommendations on three key areas: human resources management, digital government and budgeting practices.

This analysis was undertaken at the request of the Hungarian government in order to provide advice on the suitability and comprehensiveness of the PAPSDS reforms in light of the experiences of other OECD member countries.

Overall, the PAPSDS 2014-2020 is an ambitious reform programme. Its objectives are to create a public administration that supports Hungary's economic competitiveness, to improve trust in public administration by providing customer-focused services to citizens and businesses, and to make government operations more efficient. Another goal is to increase the active participation of citizens and businesses in public governance.

However, the Strategy is missing some critical elements that may hamper its chances of success: notably, it is lacking a detailed analysis of the successes and failures of previous reform efforts, and performance indicators for its main objectives.

The Strategy has, rightly, included human resources management and the development of a "digital state" as two key areas of focus. These are both critical for improving the quality of and access to public services. A professional, cost-effective, service-oriented and career-based civil service needs to be underpinned by merit-based HRM procedures and practices that link performance to rewards.

On the other hand, the review and reform of budgeting practices – crucial for improving the quality of and access to public services, is missing from both past reforms and the current Strategy.

Lessons learned from OECD countries with similar reforms could significantly improve some of Hungary's reform plans and contribute to their successful implementation. For example, there is a need for more evidence-based policy making, particularly regulatory impact assessment and giving more consideration to a range of policy options, including non-legal ones.

The report's recommendations seek to strengthen the focus on results in the civil service, notably through better human resources management practices, the use of performance indicators to better link budget decisions to results, the creation of a senior civil service cadre to enhance leadership, and improved digital government practices. These measures, by making the civil service more effective, would contribute to the success of public sector reform in Hungary.

Acknowledgements

This review would not have been possible without the support of the Hungarian officials from the Prime Minister's Office and other ministries – the Ministry of Interior and the Ministry of National Economy – who helped organise the fact finding mission to Hungary, participated in our interviews, provided key data and information and commented on earlier versions of the report.

The report was carried out under the guidance of Rolf Alter, Director, Public Governance Directorate and Edwin Lau, Head of Division, Reform of the Public Sector. It was conducted by an OECD Secretariat team led by Zsuzsanna Lonti, Senior Project Manager, who also wrote the human resources management chapter and included also Barbara Ubaldi, Senior Policy Analyst, who drafted the digital government chapter; Santiago Gonzalez, Policy Analyst who was responsible budgeting practices chapter and Beatrix Brehens, Senior Policy Analyst (seconded from the German Employment Agency), who participated in the fact finding mission and contributed to the human resources management chapter. Comments were received from Ronnie Downes, Deputy Head, Budgeting Division, Stephane Jacobzone, Deputy Head, Reform of the Public Sector Division and Daniel Gerson, Policy Analyst, Reform of the Public Sector Division.

Andrea Uhrhammer and Liv Gaunt provided editorial support. Mihaly Bak contributed to the executive summary and Liv Gaunt prepared the manuscript for publication.

Table of contents

EXECUTIVE SUMMARY 11

ASSESSMENT AND RECOMMENDATIONS 13

CHAPTER 1 25

ACHIEVEMENTS OF PREVIOUS REFORM EFFORTS – THE "MAGYARY" PROGRAMMES....... 25

Achievements of previous reforms 27
References.. 28

CHAPTER 2 29

DOES THE NEW STRATEGY SET THE RIGHT DIRECTION, THE RIGHT GUIDING PRINCIPLES AND SELECT THE RIGHT AREAS FOR INTERVENTION? 29

Guiding principles for the planning and implementation of the PAPSDS................... 30
The Vision... 34
References.. 36

CHAPTER 3 37

REFORMS OF HUMAN RESOURCES MANAGEMENT OF THE CIVIL SERVICE 37

Who are civil servants and what are their employment trends?................................. 38
What are the current human resource management (HRM) rules for civil servants? 38
What have been the key achievements in HRM from 2010-2014 and where is there a need for improvement? 40
What are the HRM reform components of the PAPSDS 2014-2020? 50
Analysis of the planned HRM reforms for 2014-2020... 52
References.. 57

CHAPTER 4 59

DIGITAL BUILDING BLOCKS OF A MODERN PUBLIC ADMINISTRATION IN HUNGARY......... 59

Introduction.. 60
Collecting and using evidence to ground policy options and broaden the digital State vision to boost competitiveness.. 60
Using data and evidence for strategic services and policies design 61
Broadening perspective and reaping benefits building on general digital readiness........ 61
Building grounds for business models and benefits realisation 62
Closing the information gap between ambitious targets and existing statistics 63
Cutting red-tape by selecting key enablers and optimising decisions for going digital.... 65
Building on achievements in administrative simplification to go digital....................... 65
Stronger governance and engagement as engines for public administration modernisation............. 73
References.. 85

CHAPTER 5 87

TOWARDS A BUDGETARY REFORM IN THE CONTEXT OF THE PUBLIC ADMINISTRATION AND PUBLIC SERVICE DEVELOPMENT STRATEGY 2014-2020 87

Linking the PAPSDS plan to the budget: the implementation of task-based budgeting 88
Making the most of task-based budgeting: performance budgeting and the audit function 90
Putting the pieces together: Improving cost accounting of existing delivery channels as the basis for the long term adoption of accrual budgeting 96
Framing the reform in such a way as to align the strategy with the constraints 97
References 101

Figures

Figure 3.1. Results from the public servants engagement survey Hungary 44
Figure 3.2. Average annual compensation of middle managers in central government 45
Figure 3.3. Average annual compensation of economists and statisticians in central government   46
Figure 3.4. Extent of the use of performance assessments in HR decisions in central government (2010) 47
Figure 3.5. Extent of the use of performance-related pay in central government (2010 48
Figure 3.6. Utilisation of strategic HRM practices in central government (2010) 53
Figure 4.1. Implementation level of key enablers in business vs citizen life events 70
Figure 4.2. Transparency across life events 2012-2013 per country (%) 74
Figure 4.3. User-centric government across life events for citizen and business life events 2012-2013 (%) 80
Figure 5.1. Use of performance budgeting practices at the central level of government (2011) 92
Figure 5.2. Standard context for developing accrual budgeting initiatives 97
Figure 5.3. Use of a medium-term perspective in the budget process (2012) 99
Figure 5.4. Elements required guaranteeing the effectiveness of a MTEF 100

Boxes

Box 2.1. The Canadian citizen-centred approach to service delivery 31
Box 2.2. Guidance on consultation: The case of the United Kingdom 32
Box 2.3. Guiding principles for open and inclusive policymaking 33
Box 2.4. Vision for the Public Administration and Public Service Development Strategy of Hungary, 2014-2020 34
Box 3.1. Merit-based recruitment in the Australian public service 41
Box 3.2. United Kingdom: Lessons from experience with performance-related pay (Hutton Review)48
Box 3.3. Setting up a Senior Public Service in Ireland 53
Box 3.4. Competency Management in the Belgian Federal Government 54
Box 4.1. Getting on the Estonian X-road – the governance process 67
Box 4.2. Estonian e-ID solution 69
Box 4.3. Belgian e-ID card 69
Box 4.4. Mandatory use of digital services in Denmark through pro-active channel management ... 71
Box 4.5. Public Sector Transparency Board: Public Data Principles 76
Box 4.6. Germany's user councils for sharing information on infrastructure and services 77
Box 4.7. Supporting learning networks and communities of practice within the Norwegian public sector 78
Box 4.8. United Kingdom government – Directgov (direct.uk.gov) 78
Box 5.1. OECD Principles on Budgetary Governance 92

Box 5.2. Accountable budget: the Dutch reform 95
Box 5.3. The medium-term perspective of the German budget process 100

Executive summary

This publication provides a brief strategic review of Hungary's Public Administration and Public Service Development Strategy 2014-2020 (hereafter referred to as the "Strategy"). The Strategy builds upon previous public sector reforms, the "Magyary Programmes 11.0 and 12.0", carried out by the Hungarian government from 2010 to 2013.

The 2014-2020 Strategy covers a longer period, in line with the European Union's development policy cycle. Its main objectives are to (1) enhance the competitiveness of the Hungarian economy by creating a well-functioning public administration, (2) improve trust in public administration by providing customer-focused public services to citizens and businesses, and (3) increase the efficiency of government operations.

This review focuses on three reform areas in particular: human resources management (HRM), digital government and budgeting practices. These areas have been selected as they are crucial to the Strategy's successful implementation.

Results of the Magyary reforms 2010-2013

The most profound change that occurred in the Hungarian public sector between 2010 and 2014 was the reorganisation of government, both at the central and territorial levels, which created a highly centralised system of public administration. The reorganisation was meant to create a more even quality of service delivery in all parts of the country and to achieve budgetary savings. However, the Strategy's status report does not provide an in-depth analysis of why notable efficiency gains for government have not yet materialised from this reorganisation, despite significant simplification and streamlining of government services.

At the same time, the 114 measures introduced to lower administrative burdens on business resulted in about HUF 500 billion in savings for businesses. However, more still needs to be done; for example, registering a business still takes considerably more time in Hungary than in neighbouring OECD countries. Progress has been made in establishing the necessary legal framework for e-government initiatives. Key achievements in HRM practices include the introduction of new job evaluation and central performance evaluation systems. Moreover, despite dissatisfaction with pay and benefits, civil servants' engagement and satisfaction rose from 58% in 2011 to 63% in 2013.

The new 2014-2020 Strategy's guiding principles include creating a stable legal environment, which is especially important given the large amount of new legislation and amendments enacted between 2010 and 2014. However, carefully conducted *ex ante* and *ex post* impact assessments should play a greater role in policy making. The Strategy also has a strong customer focus in line with its vision of a professional, cost-effective service-provider state. Finally, the Strategy refers to the principle of active citizen and business participation, which is another welcome development.

Human resources management

While there was a decrease in overall public sector employment between 2010 and 2011, this trend appears to have reversed by 2014. The Strategy has two distinct reform goals in this area: (1) the creation of a cohesive HRM system as a prerequisite for improving mobility both inside the civil service and with law enforcement and the military; and (2) the strengthening of a career-based HRM model to better attract and retain high-quality public servants. However, to achieve these goals, recruitment and promotion need to be strictly merit-based, based on competitive and standardised procedures. Such procedures are often circumvented in the Hungarian civil service. Furthermore, in order to improve the leadership capacity in the civil service, Hungary may wish to create a separate cadre of the Senior Civil Service with specific HRM practices, as in a majority of OECD member countries. Finally, in a highly delegated HRM system such as the one in Hungary, the new reforms require both strong central HRM policy direction and effective implementation on the ground.

Digital government

The Strategy also paves the way for a digital government policy in line with the OECD definition of using digital technologies as an integrated part of governments' modernisation strategies to create public value. The Strategy has four main objectives in this area: (1) increasing the efficiency and effectiveness of public service delivery; (2) improving competitiveness; (3) building trust in government; and (4) bringing public services closer to customers. However, the hard data and analytical support needed to evaluate whether the Strategy will be able to deliver on these plans is missing. This gap in information and analytical support should be filled by, for example, with use of performance information such as data about users.

To increase the take-up of digital services, the government also launched a new e-ID card in January 2016, but awareness needs to be raised among both citizens and businesses to promote the use of the card. A single access point to government information and services for all users should be created to make it easier for citizens to find the information and access services. In addition, openness, stakeholder engagement and participatory processes, enabled by digital technologies, could further improve the take-up of digital public services.

Budgeting

One crucial element missing from the new Strategy is a comprehensive budget reform linked to the other reforms. Current budgeting practices used in the Hungarian public administration are still input-based, which may have contributed to the lack of notable efficiency gains from previous reform efforts.

The 2014-2020 Strategy is accompanied by the Public Administration and Public Services Development Operational Programme 2014-2020 (PADOP) to ensure its implementation. However, the Strategy could be further strengthened by developing more detailed performance indicators for all four intervention areas.

Assessment and recommendations

This chapter starts with a brief introduction to the aims of the project followed by a brief assessment and recommendation of the past comprehensive public sector reform programmes in Hungary - the Magyary programmes. It also discusses whether the new public sector reform strategy sets the right direction for Hungary. There is a summary of the review of the three key themes of this current review of planned public sector reforms, covered in three consecutive chapters on human resources management, digital government and budgeting practices and the recommendations proposed.

Overview

This publication is the final part of the second Public Governance Review (PGR) of Hungary, which also includes a separate review of the reorganisation of the territorial administration of Hungary (OECD, 2015), as well as "Government at a Glance, how Hungary compares" (OECD, 2015), which analyses some key performance indicators of the Hungarian public administration comparing them to its neighbouring OECD member countries.

The aim of this publication is to provide a brief strategic review of Hungary's Public Administration and Public Service Development Strategy 2014-2020 (the "PAPSDS" or the "Strategy"), which was built upon the results of the previous public sector reforms of the Hungarian government from 2010 to 2013 based on the Magyary Programmes 11.0 and 12.0. These programmes have been analysed by the OECD within the framework of the first PGR of Hungary, paying special attention to the reforms related to strategic planning, fighting corruption, and creating a more citizen- and business-friendly government by way of administrative simplification and the setting up of one-stop shops. In contrast to the Magyary Programmes, the PAPSDS 2014-2020 covers a longer, seven-year period (adjusting to the European Union's development policy cycle). The new Strategy's main objectives are to (1) enhance the competitiveness of the Hungarian economy by creating a competitive public administration; (2) improve trust in public administration by providing customer-focused public services to citizens and businesses, and (3) increase the efficiency of government operations.

In agreement with the Hungarian government, this strategic review pays special attention to three reform areas: (1) human resources management (HRM), (2) digital government, and (3) budgeting practices. These areas have been selected based on their key role in the Strategy and its successful implementation.

Achievements of previous reform efforts – the "Magyary Programmes"

As an introduction to the new Strategy, a brief account of the achievements of the Magyary Programmes is provided in chapter 1. The most profound change that happened between 2010 and 2014 had been the reorganisation of Government both at the central and territorial levels, which created a highly centralised system of public administration, accompanied with significant simplification and streamlining. However, looking at the evidence provided in the new Strategy's status report, these organisational changes have not yet resulted in notable efficiency gains in terms of reduced public sector employment.

Regarding administrative simplification aimed at improving business and investor climate, some 114 measures in 10 intervention areas resulted in about HUF 500 billion in savings for businesses, according to Hungarian government sources. However, more needs to be done given that registering a business, for example, still takes considerably more time in Hungary than in neighbouring OECD countries. Concerning e-Government initiatives, there have been improvements in the legal background. In terms of human resources management (HRM) practices, the introduction of the new job evaluation and central performance evaluation systems, the establishment of the National Public Service University and the Hungarian Civil Servants Corps, as well as the introduction of the new public ethics regulation are key achievements. As a result, overall staff engagement/satisfaction of civil servants rose from 58% in 2011 to 63% in 2013, despite dissatisfaction with pay and benefits.

Recommendation : Achievements of previous reforms – The Magyary Programmes

- **Detailed analysis is needed on why reforms from 2010-2014 have brought relatively few results so far for government efficiency and for citizens.** In particular, it would be important to consider whether timelines and priorities had been realistic and whether adjustments would have been necessary. Though total public sector employment decreased somewhat between 2010 and 2011, this trend appears to have reversed by 2014. Considering improved service delivery, compared to the planned 300 one-stop shops only 102 have been set up by 2014. No information has been provided on how these organisational changes resulted in reduced inequalities in access to and quality of public services.

- The planning horizon of the new Strategy – 2014-2020 should be the time to embed those promising reforms.

Does the new strategy set the right direction for intervention?

In chapter 2 (*"Does the new strategy set the right direction, the right guiding principles and selects the right areas for intervention?"*), legal certainty is identified as a key area that requires special attention in Hungary, especially in light of the large amount of new legislation and legislative amendments enacted between 2010 and 2014. Carefully conducted ex-ante and ex-post impact assessments should play a greater role in policymaking, so as to allow policymakers to use evidence in their decision-making. The strong planned customer focus associated with the vision of a professional, cost-effective service-provider State is commendable. Moreover, the principle of active citizen and business participation is a welcomed progress for the Hungarian public administration, but appropriate guidance is needed to help create a "consultation culture" across the whole public administration. The government considers online consultations have been successful; therefore, their further application is intended; however, relying primarily on online consultation raises significant access issues. As a result, paper-based consultations are also being pursued.

Furthermore, in order to make the new Strategy successful, a detailed analysis of the causes of the previous reforms' successes and failures is necessary, since the status report included in the PAPSDS does not provide an in-depth analysis of why notable efficiency gains for government from the reorganisation of the public administration system have not yet materialised. At the same time, the selection of the management of human resources and the development of the "Digital State" among the PAPSDS's four focal areas is critical to improve both the quality of and access to public services. However, the necessary financial resources need to be provided in a transparent manner for these reforms. In that vein, one more crucial element missing both from the Magyary Programmes and the PAPSDS is the review and reform of budgeting processes (see chapter 6). Despite this shortcoming, the PAPSDS presents an ambitious reform programme, which could have been further strengthened by developing the Strategy's performance indicators in a more detailed form for all the four intervention areas.

> **Recommendation: Does the new Strategy set the right direction, the right guiding principles and select the right areas for intervention?**
>
> - **There is a need for evidence-based policymaking as part of a comprehensive policy aimed at improving regulatory design and delivery bringing together also the on-going effort to reduce administrative burdens.** This policy should provide for better consideration of alternative policy options and their impacts, carrying out proper regulatory impact assessment before legislation is enacted, better consideration on whether always a legal solution will provide the best results, and more careful drafting of legislation and regulations and quality controls on the use of these tools. Whenever appropriate, alternatives to legal solutions could be considered and impact analysis be conducted. To make the best use of capacity and resources, there should be some proportionality in the depth and scope of the analysis being conducted. The trade-offs and complementarities between efficiency and equity/fairness could be brought to the open as part of the policymaking process. In order to carry out this type of impact analysis good, detailed, pertinent data and sufficient time are needed in the policymaking process to model the impacts of various policy options.
>
> - **A comprehensive policy also needs to be developed on how active citizen and business participation mechanisms can be implemented in practice throughout the whole policy cycle,** with appropriate oversight and quality control over implementation. The speed with which laws and regulations were introduced and passed in recent years did not often provide enough time to carry out proper consultation with stakeholders. The Hungarian government is convinced that online consultations have been successful; therefore, their further application is intended. However, using primarily online consultation raises issues for those who do not have access to a computer or are not able to use it. As a result, paper-based consultations are also being pursued. Overall, there should be appropriate consideration regarding the time and platform of consultation and which mechanisms, on-line or off-line, would be most suitable for this purpose.
>
> - **Review and make more substantial the performance targets and indicators for measuring progress in all intervention areas.** A strength of the new Strategy is the inclusion of a monitoring body and the identification of an indicator system and certain targets which could be used to measure its progress. However, the role and functions of the monitoring body seem to be unclear and the indicator system contains very few performance targets. Thus it would be beneficial to set the performance targets in a more detailed form for all the four intervention areas.

Reforms of Human Resources management of the civil service

Chapter 3 (*"Reforms of human resources management of the civil service"*) focuses on the civil servants in Hungary, their employment trends, the rules pertaining to them, and the key achievements in HRM between 2010 and 2014 as well as on the areas for further improvement, before turning to the analysis of the PAPSDS's reform components for the period 2014-2020. Main findings in this chapter include that while there was some decrease in the entire public sector employment between 2010 and 2011, this trend appears to have reversed by 2014. However, despite the increase in overall staff engagement/satisfaction, there was dissatisfaction with pay, benefits and career opportunities.

Regarding the planned HRM reforms for the period 2014-2020, two distinctive goals can be observed: (1) the creation of a joined-up HRM system as a prerequisite for increased mobility not just inside civil service, but also with law enforcement and the military – the "three orders of professions", as they are called; and (2) the strengthening of the career model of HRM in order to improve the attraction and retention of the public service. A the same time, the current legislative environment and the new HRM reforms create a mix between a career- and a position-based system, becoming closer to a position-based one (which is also reflected in the introduction of a new job evaluation system, and linking it to pay).

In order to create a stronger merit-based professional civil service it is recommended that the role of competitive and standardised selection procedures be strengthened in recruitment. Furthermore, in order to increase the leadership capacity in the civil service, the creation of a separate cadre the Senior Civil Service with special HRM practices – which was observed in 23 OECD member countries in 2010, but not in Hungary – could also be considered. Finally, in a highly delegated HRM system (like the one in Hungary), the new reforms require both strong central HRM policy directions and improved implementation on the ground. However, it is not clear which organisation – the Prime Minister's Office or the Ministry of Interior – will be able to provide that central direction.

Recommendation: Reforms of human resources management of the civil service

- **The role of competitive, standardised selection procedures need to be strengthened** in civil servant recruitment. Effective mechanisms need to be developed to monitor that, in the case of restricted recruitment, the rules and standards of competitive procedure are applied. In terms of central HRM policies regarding the recruitment and selection process, the most important standard practices are the open advertisement of positions and the competitive recruitment procedures that managers need to follow. These processes are fundamental to merit-based recruitment and to avoid nepotism where recruitment and selection is based on personal loyalty. As a result, it is of the utmost importance that these be established in Hungary as well.

- **HRM rules need to be strengthened to avoid subjective evaluation and decision-making by managers** as a valid cause for termination of civil servants, as this may undermine the neutrality of the civil service as well. In an ideal environment it is also the bureaucrats' role "to speak truth to power". This is usually achieved by a clear division of labour between, on the one hand, the politicians and their political staff and, on the other hand, the bureaucrats. The policy direction is set by the politicians, while its implementation is carried out by the bureaucracy. Moreover, high turnover of civil servants counteracts the intentions of the government to build a public service career model and sends wrong signals to potential recruits.

The strategy should also include the redesign of the civil service pay system, to further link it to the requirements of the jobs using the results of job evaluation and rethink performance pay in a way that increases civil servants' motivation

Recommendation: Reforms of human resources management of the civil service
(continued)

and performance. Several OECD countries are moving away from automatic pay increases based on seniority, and movement in the salary grade is linked to the results of performance evaluations. Also, pay systems are built focusing more on the characteristics of a job. In that case job evaluation plays a key role, creating systematically a hierarchy of jobs to which pay can be linked. A rigorous job evaluation system also introduces procedural fairness into wage-setting. Moreover, a well-designed and executed job evaluation system allows identifying the key competencies for the various job families and can be used as a basis for training needs assessment, and as a useful tool to build career paths.

There is a need to strengthen strategic HRM focusing on better workforce planning and reviews and assessments of HRM capacities of organisations. This could be carried out as part of increasing the HRM capabilities. An important part of the reforms are the set-up of a core public service registration system as well as a standard personnel and monitoring system, which could form the basis of workforce

---

Recommendation: Reforms of human resources management of the civil service
(continued)

planning and the creation of the career model. However, the use of other strategic tools in HRM need to be further strengthened.

- **Consider creating a separate Senior Civil Service with special HRM practices** that **will help closer align their behaviours and performance to the Government's objectives.** Because of their strategic roles in government, there is an increased tendency among OECD countries – observed in 23 OECD countries in 2010, but not in Hungary, to group senior civil servants separately and manage them under different HRM policies. In this group greater emphasis is placed on capacity-building and on incentivising improved performance through higher portion of their remuneration being performance-related.

Digital building blocks of a modern public administration in Hungary

Chapter 4 (*"Digital building blocks of a modern public administration in Hungary"*) finds that Hungary put considerable effort in to designing the digital component of its Strategy. In fact, the PAPSDS 2014-2020 – together with the National Info-communication Strategy 2014-2020 of Hungary – is paving the way for a digital government policy that could meet the OECD definition of using "digital technologies as an integrated part of governments' modernisation strategies to create public value". The Strategy sets forth a vision of a "Digital State", aiming for a digital transformation of the public sector, which should result in (1) increased efficiency and effectiveness of public service delivery (better quality at lower costs), (2) an increase in competitiveness, (3) building trust through a customer-focused approach, and (4) bringing public services closer to customers through multichannel service delivery and 24/7 availability. However, in the absence of existing hard data and detailed analytical support, the assessment of whether the goals and indicators used are S.M.A.R.T. (specific, measurable, assignable, realistic and time-related) cannot yet be performed. Therefore, the use of performance information (including user data) in the policy design and for strategic services is recommended. Moreover, the reforms should follow different approaches based on specific target groups (to be defined on the basis of users' existing habits, level of "digital maturity" and trust).

The Strategy aims to achieve a 10% target for reducing administrative fee costs, and a 20% target for administration time and administrative burden reduction. These are ambitious goals that would require the presentation of the selected approach to achieve these targets with impact assessment and a detailed business model. Fewer, better targeted services can be an effective solution by way of a strategic selection of those services which will be available end-to-end online. In this regard, the government could build on the achievements in administrative simplification (since 2007, at least 228 administrative procedures have been reviewed and there is a tendency to categorise them according to certain criteria, among which frequency of usage is one).

Interoperability is also a key focus area of the Strategy approached from the harmonisation of databases/registers and semantics. The objective is that 80% of registers and integrated services should be deployed by 2020. In this context, the case of Estonia – where a real-time exchange platform (the X-road) has been developed – can be an interesting solution to analyse.

Regarding electronic identification solutions, the Government launched a new e-ID card in January 2016. Future steps would be required to ensure the use of the card by the public also by increasing opportunities for its use. In carrying out this task, cooperation between the central government and local governments (which are closer to citizens) should be ensured, as well as taking into account the examples of other OECD member countries, such as Belgium and Israel.

Turning to services for businesses, according to the European Commission's DESI index ("Digital economy and society index", 2014), Hungary performs below the EU average in terms of businesses' use of electronic information sharing, cloud services and social media, as well as online selling. Internet banking and online shopping in general are also below the EU average. In addition, while Hungary is among the top EU Member States regarding the general use of social networks, only about 31% of Internet users actively use e-Government services. In 2013, the reasons for not using e-Government services in Hungary were 20% due to "non-awareness of the existence of relevant websites/online services". Therefore, awareness needs to be raised both among citizens and businesses, and a single point of access for all users should be provided (such as the government portal, www.magyarorszag.hu). Also, all other websites that contain public service-related information should preferably be linked to that one single site.

Moreover, openness, stakeholders' engagement and participatory processes enabled by digital technologies can improve take-up results of digital services both in the public sector and for users of public services. Open data and a "data-driven culture" in the public sector have been recommended by the OECD. Indeed, the Strategy envisions the inclusion of users' views in the decision-making process. An ambitious target is set in that in 90% of the cases, public service providers need to run customer satisfaction surveys. On the other hand, the Strategy lacks details on how to engage stakeholders, reach out to users and "build in" their feedback into decision-making and implementation processes. The methods for engagement vary in different governments across the OECD, and Hungary needs to create its own approach.

Recommendation: Digital building blocks of a modern public administration in Hungary

- **Digitisation efforts and policy-making needs to be optimised based on strategic use of evidence.** The Government sets ambitious targets for a cost-efficient administration including a generous supply of services based on a "value for money approach" for all citizens. Nevertheless, there are several policy options to be explored which can support a more cost-efficient approach. The following are some key actions that the Government could consider taking:

- **Boost competitiveness through more informed and evidenced-based decisions.** This entails analysing existing data and statistics to identify untapped potential and map users' digital capacity and digital readiness. Presumably, use and spread of certain technologies (e.g. number of smartphone users, Internet users and social media) indicates willingness and skills availability to use digital public services. Thus, broadening the knowledge and understanding of the existing digital environment in the country can serve as a basis for a more complex self-assessment and realistic objectives-setting.

  Explore further uses of business case models to improve results. The government could develop, adopt and apply a business case methodology which better takes into account a broader set of criteria that sustain the selection of projects supporting a whole-of-government perspective. The aim would be to bridge the gaps between citizen and business interests on one side, and the government's view in the choice of the digital solutions on the other. There is an overall need to provide details on how impact assessments, benchmarking, business models or other methodologies support the selection of policy directions and implementation.

Recommendation: Digital building blocks of a modern public administration in Hungary *(continued)*

- **Make more strategic use of data to prioritise digitalisation of public services** Use the administrative portal (www.magyarorszag.hu) statistics more strategically, and collect and refer to data extracted from the multichannel services. Provide details on types and related priorities, e.g. which ones are fully transactional. Details could also be provided on the plans for digital transition for specific services clarifying the expected timeline. The Government may consider including a mechanism in the monitoring and evaluation process to refer to service types and benchmark their use as an input for optimal policy decisions.

- **Cutting red-tape by selecting key enablers and optimising decisions for going digital implies taking a number of integrated actions, from technical, legal and substantive perspectives**. As many steps have been taken, there is momentum to optimise both policy and budgetary decisions building on previous investments to deliver more visible results to the users. Some of the work has already been completed and information lacks mainly on the implementation side. The actions suggested below are specific steps the government may consider taking:

- **Build on past developments to take interoperability to the next level and deliver more visible results for users**

- **Build on achievements on procedural, legal and technical issues (e.g. information on reviewed services, created taxonomies and e-document practice) and create space for parallel testing and developments**. Communicate the selected services efficiently to the users and scale them up gradually to become digital entirely. For instance, there is a need for a clear implementation plan for interoperability clarifying different aspects (legal, technical, organisational and semantic solutions). Testing, which is ongoing for many services that will be available online in 2016, has been helpful to understand what needs to be further developed to satisfy broader reform needs.

- **Maximise potential arising from the introduction of the new e-ID solution and consider complementary cloud services.** This includes selecting key enablers and analysing policy choices to support timely decisions on developments of highest priority (e.g. secure electronic ID and authentication when using a broad range of public and related private services). This should take into account the emergence and spread of new business models (e.g. cloud computing, smartphone applications) to complement the actions of the Government. This should include potential incentives that drive both administration and business to benefit more from both cloud and shared services.

- **Strengthen the one-stop-shop portal for online public services** by keeping the good practice of providing one single point of access and consider business continuity and change management when introducing any new solution to ensure trust and better user experience.

  Focus on targeted take-up of digital services. Consider performing and presenting the definition of a vision and policy options on its implementation based on user take-up targets. Apply quantitative targets (e.g. certain percentage of 1 - Population, 2 - Internet users, 3 - Client Gate registered users to use by specific dates digital services). Consider mandatory policy as an option for those that are ready by adopting a "stick and carrot" strategy for certain digital services (e.g. businesses) and scaling them up while preventing digital exclusion. Clearly, the approach towards a "digital-by-default" service delivery, resting on a mandatory targeting of those users who can use digital tools should be introduced, while maintaining a careful approach that takes into account personal preferences. **There is a need to build up a governance framework**

> **Recommendation: Digital building blocks of a modern public administration in Hungary** *(continued)*:
>
> - **to support better co-ordination and stakeholders' engagement.** Focus on strengthening governance and engagement engines is essential, as the reorganization of institutional structures and governance frameworks can have an important impact on efficiency and effectiveness of implementation and results. Open data and new online collaborative platforms for stakeholders' engagement inspired by principles of openness and transparency can for instance produce strategic new business models to improve the offer of digital services and better meet different users' needs. The government could consider taking the specific actions below:
>
> - **Improve institutional co-ordination and collaboration processes and governance mechanisms.** Consider reviewing the existing governance framework for digital government to clarify the list of responsibilities and task allocation for all key actors. Create the necessary dynamics and mechanisms to ensure efficient co-ordination in the definition and implementation of a whole-of-government digital State vision. Describe in relevant documents, at forums and also on the web the relevant institutional co-ordination processes and governance mechanisms in a way that enables any interested public organisation to notice its role and contribute to the Strategy's implementation. This should also lead to better co-ordinated, harmonised and more legitimate/accepted decisions, which increase efficiency, sense of ownership and trust.
>
>   **Contemplate open government as an option.** Elaborate on the aspect of openness, and specifically on the opportunity open government brings to the administration. Consider developing a flexible governance framework, which allows for a strong co-ordination within the Government on "what must be done" (e.g. certain technical solutions) while at the same time bringing up a whole digital government ecosystem (including businesses, NGOs, citizens) to offer solutions on "what needs to happen" (e.g. digital transition). Focus on developing a strategy towards open data policy in order to extend options for implementing new business models and fostering a "data-driven culture" within the public sector.
>
> - **Plan stakeholders' engagement** and benefit from closer co-operation through modern tools and approaches. The government may consider including (1) a communication and strategic engagement plan (e.g. with targeted initiatives such as the Danish e-Day initiative), or (2) a social media strategy (e.g. UK, US), or (3) generating innovative service co-creation in partnership with different stakeholders (e.g. like in the UK). Additionally, evidence could be given on stakeholders' consultation and on how the Government is opening up during the policymaking process to support increased uptake of the new opportunities.

Towards a budgetary reform

Finally, chapter 5 (*"Towards a budgetary reform in the context of the public administration and public service reform strategy 2014-2020"*) focuses on one crucial element missing from the Strategy: the implementation of a comprehensive budget reform, which could be linked to the other reforms envisaged in the Strategy. Following the recommendations by the EU, Hungary has recently undertaken adjustments to its budgetary process – notably, strengthening the planning horizon beyond the current budget year to incorporate 3 years ahead. However, the binding nature of this extended framework is still to be assessed.

Moreover, current budgeting practices used in Hungarian public administration are still input-based (within the framework of a traditional line-item budget, which is structured along the lines of organisational units and spending categories). This could have contributed to the lack of notable efficiency gains to be realised by the previous

Magyary Programmes. In that environment, efficiency gains can only be achieved by top-down budget cuts, where their magnitude is set arbitrarily and without sufficient budgetary information from the "ground". Hungary is thus missing a crucial opportunity with the changes in how public services are delivered (both through organisational changes and with the creation of one-stop shops) to introduce rigorous cost accounting for the various services. Those cost accounting practices could, in turn, form the basis for the introduction of task-based budgeting, and – over time – performance budgeting. The OECD Principles on Budgetary Governance, as set out in the 2015 recommendations on budgetary governance, are based upon the notion of inter-connected, mutually supportive elements of the overall budgetary framework, and therefore could be considered as a valuable input to a Hungarian process of budgetary reform.

Recommendation: Towards a budgetary reform in the context of the Public Administration and Public Service Development Strategy 2014-2020

- **Implementing task-based budgeting would be welcomed** as an efficient channel to modernise the budgetary process and achieve efficiency gains, and a clear timeline and comprehensive working plan should be set for the adoption of task-based budgeting. The introduction of task-based budgeting would require important changes in the budgetary culture and major realignment of the budgetary process. The task inventory created under the Magyary Programmes could be a good starting point. The Hungarian government is encouraged to set a clear timeline and action plan for implementation. Furthermore, all relevant stakeholders should be invited to analyse the scope and implications of adopting this budgeting system. Effective implementation should consider that tasks and sub-tasks must be results-based and indicators to measure its achievement should be designed. Moreover, tasks should be aligned with government-wide policy priorities, and should be kept as simple as possible. Finally, the Ministry of Finance could create a special unit to provide support services to other ministries and agencies in establishing and aligning their tasks and common indicators. The selection of one representative set of tasks involving different spending units could be considered as a pilot experience that would serve as the starting point for the gradual implementation of task-based budgeting.

- **The implementation of task-based budgeting should be accompanied by the introduction of the right performance budgeting framework.** It should be designed in such a way that performance information could be used as a context for the financial allocations within the budget. The supreme audit institution should be integrated within the performance framework. More than half of OECD countries have standard performance budgeting frameworks in place which apply to all central government line ministries and agencies. In the OECD Principles on Budgetary Governance (adopted in 2015), it is mentioned that performance information should be presented in a way that provides useful context for the financial allocations in the budget report.

- **The current changes in the service delivery scheme provide a window of opportunity to improve cost accounting;** in turn, enhanced cost information could be used to nurture the performance system required in the context of task-based budgeting. However, in the long term, the objective should be the adoption of an accrual budgeting system. Reforms towards the adoption of accrual budgeting seek to keep managers responsible for all costs associated with the outcomes/outputs produced, not just the immediate cash outlays. Enhanced information on costs could set the stage for the adoption of an accrual-based budgeting system as a longer-term objective. This process is only recommended when accompanied by a developed system of performance management and budgeting. Hence, an accrual budgeting system should only be put in place once the necessary capacities have been reached. In the absence of these, it is prudent for countries to continue upgrading their existing cash-based systems.

- **There is a need to harmonise policy strategies and the budget decisions by guaranteeing the binding nature of the medium-term budgetary framework.** Hungary has recently moved in the direction of incorporating a medium-term perspective (three years ahead) into the budgetary process. In order to fully benefit from this planning tool the existence of solid political commitment towards fiscal sustainability is crucial. Moreover, in order to enhance the binding nature of the framework it is necessary to strengthen ex-post monitoring of compliance with the fiscal rules and be committed to the use of corrective mechanisms if necessary.

Chapter 1

Achievements of previous reform efforts – the "Magyary" programmes

This chapter provides a brief strategic review of Hungary's Public Administration and Public Service Development Strategy. It continues with a brief analysis of the status report included in Hungary's Public Administration and Public Service Development Strategy, enumerating the major achievements and shortcomings of the "Magyary programmes" carried out from 2011 - 2013. It touches upon the aims and results of the reorganisation of both the central and territorial administration in Hungary; administrative simplification; e-government; and some key aspects of human resources management reforms.

The aim of this publication is to provide a brief strategic review of the Public Administration and Public Service Development Strategy (PAPSDS) of Hungary, 2014-2020. This strategy is built upon the results of previous public sector reforms of the Hungarian government during the period 2010-2013: the Magyary Programmes 11.0 and 12.0. The OECD has provided an analysis of the Magyary Programmes as part of the first Hungarian Public Governance Review (PGR) paying special attention to the reforms aimed at strategic planning; fighting corruption; and creating a more citizen- and business-friendly government by way of administrative simplification and one-stop shops. The first review also included a short analysis of the reforms to the territorial administration (OECD, 2015a).

The current strategic review is part of the second PGR of Hungary, which also includes the separate review of the reorganisation of the territorial administration of Hungary, the most important and far-reaching part of the public administration reforms carried out since 2010, moving from a highly fragmented territorial administration to a highly integrated, but at the same time deconcentrated one (OECD, 2015b). As a result, those issues that relate to the reorganisation of territorial administration will not be addressed in this strategic review. This second PGR also encompasses the "Hungarian Government at a Glance", a separate publication, which compares some key performance indicators of the Hungarian public administration to its neighbouring OECD member countries – the Czech Republic, the Slovak Republic, Poland, Estonia, Slovenia, Austria and Germany (OECD, 2015c). There is also a brief comparative report forthcoming on the international indicators and benchmarking practices developed for public administrations.

The PAPSDS 2014-2020 covers a longer, seven-year period - adjusting to the European Union's development policy cycle - than the previous Magyary Programmes that matched the length of the Government's mandate from 2010-2014. The new strategy's main strategic objectives are:

- enhancing the competitiveness of the Hungarian economy by creating a competitive public administration;

- improving trust in public administration by providing customer-focused public services to citizens and businesses; and

- increasing the efficiency of government operations.

The main areas the strategy focuses on are: the conclusion of organisational reforms started in 2011, affecting both the central and territorial public administration; the development of human resources and their management; improving the standards of public services, including better organisational conditions, red-tape reduction and the use of e-government; and digitizing state and public services, managed and supported by digital back-office workflows. It also includes the creation of a monitoring system and a set of indicators with targets to be achieved by the new strategy.

In agreement with the Hungarian government this OECD strategic review pays special attention to three areas of reform:
1. human resources management;

2. digital government; and
3. budgeting practices.

While some of these topics have also been discussed in the previous OECD review, they have not been the primary focus of that analysis. These areas have been selected based on their key role in the strategy and its successful implementation.

Achievements of previous reforms

As an introduction to the new strategy a brief account of the achievements of the previous Magyary Programmes is provided, comparing the performance of the Hungarian public administration on a few competitiveness indicators to other neighbouring countries, as well as to the objectives of the Magyary Programmes. The status report included in the PAPSDS is more output- than outcome-focused, enumerating primarily the various reform actions of the Hungarian government but where data are available, also the results of those actions.

The most profound change that happened between 2010 and 2014 had been the reorganisation of government both at the central and territorial levels. The reorganisation created a highly centralised system of public administration with eight "super-ministries" at the central level, accompanied with significant reduction, simplification and reorganisation of the system of foundations and public endowments and the streamlining of the system of government offices, central offices and support institutions. In addition, a new, integrated but deconcentrated territorial public administration replaced the previously highly fragmented territorial administration. These changes resulted in a high concentration of power and resources at the central level of government and its deconcentrated organs. The major objectives of this reorganisation were to improve efficiency of operations and ensure that the quality and access to public services will be similar across the whole country.

Looking at the evidence provided in the status report, these organisational changes have not yet resulted in notable efficiency gains in terms of reduced public sector employment. Considering improved service delivery, compared to the planned 300 one-stop shops only 102 have been set up by 2013, handling 256 administrative procedures. However, the establishment of district offices and their formation as back-offices constituted the organisational background for the set-up of one-stop shops, called "government windows" in Hungary. No information has been provided on how these organisational changes resulted in reduced inequalities in access to and quality of public services across the country by the end of 2014, our review period.

Regarding administrative simplification aimed at improving business and investor climate, some 114 measures in 10 intervention areas have been carried out for businesses, which resulted in approximately HUF 500 billion in savings for businesses. In response to these measures, Hungary expects a 1.2-1.3% increase in GDP in the long run, and a significant improvement in competitiveness. However, more needs to be done. According to the OECD's Product Market Regulation (PMR) indicator, the registration of a business still takes 4 times longer in Hungary than in Slovakia, and this gap is even greater in relation to the rest of the neighbouring countries. The registration of a share company takes 35 days in Hungary; more than twice as many as in the Czech Republic. According to the World Bank's Doing Business Index, in Hungary 24 procedures were required for the acquisition of planning permission in

2013, while this number is 18 on average in the countries of the region, and 13 in the OECD countries.

Regarding e-government initiatives there have been improvements in the legal background – which changed from an excessively centralised system to a modular approach – and to the quality of e-services as well. There have been modifications to several acts enabling e-procedures and the introduction of a new legislation on interoperability and the creation and definition of regulated e-services as key building blocks of e-administration. In terms of improved e-services the Government's administrative client service centre and hotline (1818 and 1818.hu) is worth mentioning, as well as the educational and awareness programmes launched on e-services to citizens. In addition, an Application Service Provider (ASP) centre for electronic services provided for and by local municipalities has been launched.

In terms of human resources management practices the piloting of the new job evaluation system, the introduction of the central performance evaluation system, the establishment of the National Public Service University and the Hungarian Civil Servants Corps, and the introduction of the new public ethics regulation are key achievements.

All these developments resulted in improvements of overall staff engagement/satisfaction for civil servants. It has been measured in 2008, 2011 and 2013. In 2008 engagement levels of civil servants were at 40%; in 2011 at 58%, a very large improvement, and in 2013 at 63%. Engagement of management has been higher at 73%. At the same time, there has been great dissatisfaction among staff with pay, benefits and career opportunities in the Hungarian public administration.

Recommendation: *Detailed analysis is needed on why reforms have brought relatively few results so far. In particular, it would be important to consider whether timelines and priorities had been realistic and whether adjustments are needed. This might be the time to embed those promising reforms.*

REFERENCES

OECD (2015a), *Hungary: Towards a Strategic State Approach*, OECD Public Governance Reviews, OECD Publishing. http://dx.doi.org/10.1787/9789264213555-en

OECD (2015b), *Hungary: Reforming the State Territorial Administration*, OECD Public Governance Reviews, OECD Publishing, Paris. http://dx.doi.org/10.1787/9789264232921-en

OECD (2015c), *Government at a Glance: How Hungary Compares*, OECD Publishing, Paris. http://dx.doi.org/10.1787/9789264233720-en

Chapter 2

Does the new strategy set the right direction, the right guiding principles and select the right areas for intervention?

The guiding principles and the vision of the new Public Administration and Public Service strategy is examined in this chapter. The need for a stable legal environment for economic development is discussed; as well as the requirement to carry out impact assessments before policy interventions, including the analysis of distributional effects of suggested policies. Various ways for meaningful citizen and business participation in policy making is also considered together with human resources management practices to ensure a capable, motivated and dedicated workforce. The lack of planned budgeting reforms is also questioned.

Guiding principles for the planning and implementation of the PAPSDS

In order to achieve the stated objectives of the reforms Hungary intends to create a public administration that is highly professional, customer-centred, and efficient. The planning and implementation of the strategy adhere to the following principles:

- all proposed actions need to be vetted from the viewpoint of their impact on competitiveness;

- pursuing a combination of tools to achieve societal goals;

- customer-centricity to improve trust;

- active participation of citizens and businesses; and

- the creation of a fair and efficient public administration.

While these main principles are rooted very much in the Hungarian context, they are also pursued by many OECD countries' public administrations. Creating a public administration that contributes to the competitiveness of the Hungarian economy is essential both for economic growth and societal well-being. Tools mentioned to achieve that include improved efficiency of operations, the creation of a liveable and transparent business and investor climate by way of reduced administrative burdens, better organised service delivery and a stable legal environment. The reduction of administrative burdens has been analysed in great detail by the PGR and service delivery is addressed by the territorial review as well as the digital government part of this review (OECD 2015)a); OECD (2015)b).

From these, legal certainty requires special attention in Hungary. As the Hungarian public administration follows a strong legal tradition, laws are keys to its operation. However, the enactment of a very large amount of new legislation, more than 1,000 in 2011 alone, and the frequent amendments to existing laws and regulations that happened between 2010 and 2014 had profound implications both for the economy and society. It negatively affected the business climate by creating uncertainty and increasing the cost of operating a business in Hungary. This has been an especially acute problem for small and medium-sized businesses that might not be able to afford hiring extra staff to follow all the legal changes affecting their business. As a result, investor confidence has also been reduced, both foreign and national, and consequently the competitiveness of Hungary has been negatively affected. The great number of legal changes is partly justified by the large volume of transformations carried out in all sectors. At the same time, the number of amendments to legislation has decreased during the last two years, improving somewhat the legal certainty.

There has also often been haste in the legislative process and use of fast-track procedures, resulting in limited analysis of the impacts of the proposed legislation and constant revisions to even newly enacted legislation, mainly due to hurried and faulty drafting. The speed with which laws and regulations have been introduced and passed did not leave enough time to carrying out proper impact assessments and consultation with stakeholders, thereby creating unforeseen or unintended consequences of policies, which, in turn, generated the need for policy and legislative corrections later (OECD (2015a).

This problem might also be eased by the principle of pursuing a carefully selected combination of tools, among them alternatives to legal solutions.

In addition, impact assessments could take into consideration distributional impacts. The trade-offs and complementarities between efficiency and equity/fairness need to be brought to the open as part of the policymaking process, so that this evidence is available to policymakers. In order to carry out this type of impact analysis good, detailed, pertinent data and sufficient time are needed in the policymaking process to model the impacts of various policy options.

Recommendation: *There is a need for evidence-based policymaking as part of a comprehensive policy aimed at improving regulatory design and delivery bringing together also the on-going effort to reduce administrative burden. This policy should provide for better consideration of alternative policy options and their impacts, carrying out proper regulatory impact assessment before legislation is enacted, better consideration on whether always a legal solution will provide the best results, and more careful drafting of legislation and regulations and quality controls on the use of these tools.*

Having a strong customer focus with the creation of a "servicing State" is commendable. While improving the quality of public services is paramount and all OECD governments strive for it, there is a division among countries in terms of whether they look at public services from a customer or from a citizen perspective. Having a customer focus represents a more business-like approach to public services, while having a citizen focus puts the emphasis on having good quality public services as a right attached to being a citizen.

Box 2.1. The Canadian citizen-centred approach to service delivery

The Canadian approach to service improvement in the public sector has consistently described itself as "citizen-centred". The collaborative institution established by the Canadian service delivery community is called the Institute for Citizen-Centred Service.

In 1998, the Canadian government conducted the first in the series of Citizens First surveys aimed at discovering what citizens thought about the delivery of public services. That initial Citizens First survey determined the level of citizens' satisfaction with public sector service delivery by analysing over three thousand recent service experiences across a range of programs and channels. It found that there were five "drivers" of satisfaction which accounted for over seventy percent of the service satisfaction outcome in the public sector:

1. Timeliness
2. Knowledge and competence
3. Courtesy
4. Fairness
5. Outcome

Based on those results, the goal of the Service Improvement Initiative is to improve Canadians' satisfaction with the quality of Government of Canada services. To achieve this, the Initiative provides departments and agencies a framework for service delivery improvement which adopts a citizen's 'outside-in' perspective, is results-based, and is anchored in clients' own service expectations and improvement priorities.

Three main reasons explain the use of the term "citizen-centred" rather than "client-centred"

Box 2.1 The Canadian citizen-centred approach to service delivery *(continued)*

approach. Firstly, the Canadian approach acknowledges that "clients" of government services are not "just" clients, as they might be in the private sector. They are not just consumers of government services. They are usually also taxpayers and citizens, that is: bearers of rights and duties in the framework of a democratic community. As taxpayers and members of a civic or democratic community, citizens "own" the organisations that provide public services, and have civic interests that go well beyond their own service needs.

Secondly, the Canadian approach acknowledges that clients of government are "involuntary clients," whose service relationship with government derives not from choice but rather from their obligations as citizens, or from the rights of other citizens. That is one reason why "fairness" is among the five top drivers of Canadians' satisfaction with the quality of government service delivery.

Thirdly, those who deliver government services may have to balance the distinct interests and needs of different categories of citizens, within the broader framework of the public interest. They may also have to balance the interests of immediate or direct clients with those of the citizens of Canada as a whole. The Canadian citizen-centred approach therefore acknowledges that the satisfaction of immediate "clients" needs to go hand in hand with the confidence of all citizens in the institutions of government.

Source: Institute for Citizen-Centred Service (consulted on the 25th March, 2015: http://www.iccs-isac.org/en/about/service.htm).

The principle of active citizen and business participation has been raised in the first strategic review of the Magyary Programmes as an important missing element of that strategy. It is the basic ingredient of open and transparent governance, without which neither good public policymaking nor good quality of public service delivery can be envisaged, and, as a result, it is a welcomed progress for the Hungarian public administration.

The devil is in the detail: how it will be implemented in practice. At what stages in the policymaking process will participation be sought? Whose opinion and how will be canvassed? How will those opinions be reflected in the final decision-making process? Will citizen participation apply to service design and delivery as well? In this regard the development of this strategy has been a good example, as it has been the subject of wide consultations both inside and outside government. Appropriate guidance can help streamline a "consultation culture" across the public administration.

Box 2.2. Guidance on consultation: The case of the United Kingdom

Prior to replacing it with the much shorter "Consultation Principles" in 2012, the United Kingdom had a detailed "Code of Practice on Consultation", which aimed to "help improve the transparency, responsiveness and accessibility of consultations, and help in reducing the burden of engaging in government policy development."

Although not legally binding and only applying to formal, written consultations, the Code of Practice constitutes a good example of how a government can provide its civil servants with a powerful tool to improve the consultation process. The 16-page Code of Practice is divided into seven criteria, which were to be reproduced as shown below in every consultation.

- Criterion 1. When to consult
  Formal consultation should take place at a stage when there is scope to influence the policy outcome.

- Criterion 2. Duration of consultation exercises
  Consultations should normally last for at least 12 weeks with consideration given to longer timescales where feasible and sensible.

> **Box 2.2. Guidance on consultation: The case of the United Kingdom** *(continued)*
>
> - Criterion 3. Clarity of scope and impact
>   Consultation documents should be clear about the consultation process, what is being proposed, the scope to influence and the expected costs and benefits of the proposals.
>
> - Criterion 4. Accessibility of consultation exercises
>   Consultation exercises should be designed to be accessible to, and clearly targeted at, those people the exercise is intended to reach.
>
> - Criterion 5. The burden of consultation
>   Keeping the burden of consultation to a minimum is essential if consultations are to be effective and if consultees' buy-in to the process is to be obtained.
>
> - Criterion 6. Responsiveness of consultation exercises
>   Consultation responses should be analysed carefully and clear feedback should be provided to participants following the consultation.
>
> - Criterion 7. Capacity to consult
>   Officials running consultations should seek guidance in how to run an effective consultation exercise and share what they have learned from the experience.
>
> *Sources:* www.bis.gov.uk/files/file47158.pdf for the 2008 Code of Practice on Consultation and www.gov.uk/government/uploads/system/uploads/attachment_data/file/60937/Consultation-Principles.pdf for the 2012 Consultation Principles, which replaced the 2008 Code of Practice.

The Hungarian government regards online consultations as having been successful; therefore, their further application is intended. Their main advantage is good quality information that can be relatively easily analysed. However, using primarily only online consultation raises access issues for those who do not have access to a computer or are not able to use it. As a result, paper-based consultations are also being pursued.

Recommendation: *A comprehensive policy needs to be developed on how active citizen and business participation mechanisms can be implemented in practice throughout the whole policy cycle with appropriate oversight and quality controls over its implementation.*

> **Box 2.3. Guiding principles for open and inclusive policymaking**
>
> 1. *Commitment:* Leadership and strong commitment to open and inclusive policymaking is needed at all levels – politicians, senior managers and public officials.
>
> 2. *Rights:* Citizens' rights to information, consultation and public participation in policymaking and service delivery must be firmly grounded in law or policy. Government obligations to respond to citizens must be clearly stated. Independent oversight arrangements are essential to enforcing these rights.
>
> 3. *Clarity:* Objectives for, and limits to, information, consultation and public participation should be well-defined from the outset. The roles and responsibilities of all parties must be clear. Government information should be complete, objective, reliable, relevant, and easy to find and understand.
>
> 4. Time: Public engagement should be undertaken as early in the policy process as

---

Box 2.3. Guiding principles for open and inclusive policymaking *(continued)*

possible to allow a greater range of solutions and to raise the chances of successful implementation. Adequate time must be available for consultation and participation to be effective.

5. *Inclusion:* All citizens should have equal opportunities and multiple channels to access information, be consulted and participate. Every reasonable effort should be made to engage with as wide a variety of people as possible.

6. *Resources:* Adequate financial, human and technical resources are needed for effective public information, consultation and participation. Government officials must have access to appropriate skills, guidance and training as well as an organisational culture that supports both traditional and online tools.

7. *Co–ordination:* Initiatives to inform, consult and engage civil society should be co-ordinated within and across levels of government to ensure policy coherence, avoid duplication and reduce the risk of "consultation fatigue". Co-ordination efforts should not stifle initiative and innovation but should leverage the power of knowledge networks and communities of practice within and beyond government.

8. *Accountability:* Governments have an obligation to inform participants how they use inputs received through public consultation and participation. Measures to ensure that the policymaking process is open, transparent and amenable to external scrutiny can help increase accountability of, and trust in, government.

9. *Evaluation:* Governments need to evaluate their own performance. To do so effectively will require efforts to build the demand, capacity, culture and tools for evaluating public participation.

10. *Active citizenship:* Societies benefit from a dynamic civil society, and governments can facilitate access to information, encourage participation, raise awareness, strengthen citizens' civic education and skills, as well as to support capacity-building among civil society organisations. Governments need to explore new roles to effectively support autonomous problem-solving by citizens, CSOs and businesses.

Sources:
OECD (2001), *Citizens as Partners: Information, Consultation and Public Participation in Policy Making*, OECD Publishing, Paris, http://dx.doi.org/10.1787/9789264195561-en, updated in OECD (2009); *Focus on Citizens: Public Engagement for Better Policy and Services*, OECD Studies on Public Engagement, OECD Publishing, Paris, http://dx.doi.org/10.1787/9789264048874-en.

The Vision

The vision of the new strategy is the creation of a professional, cost-effective service-provider State. In order to achieve that four areas have been selected for action: (1) development of the organisational conditions of a service-provider public administration; (2) improved management of the human resources of public administration; (3) improvement of the standard of public services, and (4) development of the "digital State".

Box 2.4. Vision for the Public Administration and Public Service Development Strategy of Hungary, 2014-2020

"It is our objective that Hungarian public administration should operate by 2020 in an organised, consistent and transparent institutional structure with advanced, customer-friendly

---

> **Box 2.4. Vision for the Public Administration and Public Service Development Strategy of Hungary 2014-2020** *(continued)*
>
> procedures, should be fully accessible to all, should rely on a professional, highly qualified, ethical and motivated workforce with a national calling, and should function cost-effectively, within a sophisticated organisational framework, with the lowest possible administrative costs, competitive service fees and short administration deadlines. In other words, we seek to create a SERVICE PROVIDER STATE which enjoys the trust of the people." (PMO Hungary, 2015)

This vision of the Hungarian State as a service provider includes some fundamental good governance principles such as consistent and transparent institutional structure, with advanced customer-friendly procedures fully accessible to all, with a professional, ethical workforce providing services cost-effectively. But envisioning a State solely as a service provider limits its responsibilities considerably. While it is important "what" governments produce, "how" they are produced is equally important beyond technically competent, fully accessible and cost-effective delivery.

There is a need for a detailed analysis of the causes of the successes and failures of the previous reforms to guide the new strategy. The status report included in the strategy carries that task out only in a limited way. For example, it does not provide an in-depth analysis of why efficiency gains from the reorganisation have not yet materialised nor does it show data on how customer satisfaction with public services evolved. As a result, there is has been no evaluation of the impact of the far-reaching organisational changes that happened during the period 2010-2014 by the end of this period. At the same time this information will be crucial before new organisational changes and further centralisation of the Hungarian public administration occur.

However, as a key ingredient to successful public sector reforms is a committed workforce, the selection of the management of human resources for further intervention is crucial. The Magyary Programmes also included important reforms regarding how human resources are managed and developed in the public sector, which has already been described briefly in chapter 2. The same argument applies to focusing on the digital State. Information and communication technology developments also have profound implications on both how the back-office and the front-office operates and is expected to lead to efficiency gains in public administration and to more convenient and improved service delivery by way of how government interacts with citizens and businesses. ICT technologies could also improve openness in public administration, which, in turn, could be the basis of better accountability in the public sector. Reforms in human resources management and in the introduction of the digital State could both be aimed at improving the quality and the accessibility of public services.

There is a crucial element missing from both the previous Magyary Programmes and the new development strategy, and that is the review and reform of budgeting practices. Current budgeting practices in Hungarian public administration are still input-based, which could have contributed to the lack of efficiency gains to be realised by the previous Magyary Programmes. In that environment efficiency gains can be achieved only by top-down budget cuts where their magnitude is set arbitrarily and without sufficient budgetary information from the "ground". Hungary is missing a crucial opportunity with the changes on how services are delivered, both through organisational changes and with the set-up of one-stop shops, to introduce rigorous cost accounting. Those cost accounting practices could, in turn, form the basis of the introduction of task-based budgeting and, over time, performance budgeting.

The new development strategy presents an ambitious reform programme, which is accompanied by the Public Administration and Public Services Development Operational Programme 2014-2020 (PADOP) that serves the execution and implementation of the PAPSDS 2014-2020 strategy.

A strength of the new Strategy is the inclusion of a monitoring body and the identification of an indicator system and certain targets which could be used to measure its progress. However, the role and functions of the monitoring body seem to be unclear and the indicator system contains very few performance targets. Thus it would be beneficial to develop the performance targets in a more detailed form for all the four intervention areas.

Recommendation: *Review and make more substantial the performance targets and indicators for measuring progress in all intervention areas.*

REFERENCES

OECD (2001), *Citizens as Partners: Information, Consultation and Public Participation in Policy Making*, OECD Publishing, Paris, http://dx.doi.org/10.1787/9789264195561-en, updated in OECD (2009); *Focus on Citizens: Public Engagement for Better Policy and Services*, OECD Studies on Public Engagement, OECD Publishing, Paris, http://dx.doi.org/10.1787/9789264048874-en

OECD (2015a), *Hungary: Towards a Strategic State Approach*, OECD Public Governance Reviews, OECD Publishing. http://dx.doi.org/10.1787/9789264213555-en

OECD (2015b), *Hungary: Reforming the State Territorial Administration*, OECD Public Governance Reviews, OECD Publishing, Paris. http://dx.doi.org/10.1787/9789264232921-en

OECD (2015c), Regulatory Policy Outlook 2015, OECD Publishing, Paris. DOI: http://dx.doi.org/10.1787/9789264238770-en

2008 Code of Practice on Consultation www.bis.gov.uk/files/file47158.pdf

2012 Consultation Principles, which replaced the 2008 Code of Practice. www.gov.uk/government/uploads/system/uploads/attachment_data/file/60937/Consultation-Principles.pdf

Chapter 3

Reforms of human resources management of the civil service

A thorough investigation of the human resources management reforms between 2010-2013 as well as the planned reforms are provided in this chapter which evaluates whether the requirements for a merit based, neutral, professional government workforce are established in Hungary. This entails a description and enumeration of the public sector workforce, as well as the practices and reforms plans related to recruitment and selection, job evaluation, performance evaluation, remuneration, promotion and dismissal. The special human resources management practices for the senior civil service are investigated, as well as the dissatisfaction of public servants with pay and benefits.

The implementation of public sector reforms and the achievement of their objectives depend on the skills, knowledge, motivation and commitment of the public sector workforce that have to carry them out. Whether people with the right skills and knowledge will be attracted and retained, how they will perform and whether they will be motivated to carry out the reform goals is, in turn, dependent on the human resources management practices that are instituted by the Government. This chapter reviews the existing human resources management practices – including the reforms implemented between 2010 and 2013, and the human resources management reforms planned for the 2014-2020 period – in order to evaluate whether they will be sufficient to achieve the main objectives of the future reforms and address the major human resource challenges the Hungarian civil service is facing.

Who are civil servants and what are their employment trends?

In the Hungarian public sector there are several categories of public employees. There are public servants working for the central and territorial levels of public administration, namely in ministries, central and territorial level agencies, as well as in municipalities and independent agencies. Their number in July 2013 was 118,853. There are the employees in uniformed services – police, intelligence services and the army –; those with special constitutional status – judges, prosecutors and political appointees –; and other public servants – nurses, doctors, teachers, social workers, etc. of public institutions. There are approximately 0.5 million public servants (The Civil Service System in Hungary, 2014). The human resources management component of the PAPSDS of Hungary 2014-2020 focuses primarily on the management of public servants and those in uniformed services.

Since 2010 the public servants are further divided into two groups: government officials, those working under the ultimate hierarchical control of the Cabinet – ministries, central agencies and their regional units – and all others, who are "non-cabinet public servants" - e.g. working for municipalities and independent agencies. Some of the human resources management rules and practices are different for these two groups of civil servants. Our main focus in this report is on the "government officials".

The organisational reforms that have taken place between 2010 and 2013 in Hungary had a large impact on the existing workforce. New ministries have been created while old ones got abolished, and the system of government offices, central offices and support institutions has been streamlined in order to eliminate duplication and anomalies in the distribution of resources and responsibilities, with the major goal of improved utilisation of human resources. In addition, staff consolidation plans were also implemented, at ministries and their support institutions, including the termination of unfilled vacancies. However, due to other institutional reforms, while there was some decrease in the entire public sector employment between 2010 and 2011, this trend appears to have reversed by 2014. Following the reorganisation of the responsibilities of state administration and local governments, the number of those working in the municipal sector decreased between 2011 and 2013 in proportion to the rise in the number of those working in central public administration. The number of municipal employees started rising once again between 2013 and 2014.

What are the current human resource management (HRM) rules for civil servants?

As part of the public sector reforms from 2010-2013 new human resources management rules were established by the end of 2011 with the new Public Officials Act

(No. 199/2011). The new Act replaced the 1992 Civil Service Code, which itself has been modified more than a hundred times. The 2011 Act is comprehensive and it covers all key aspects of human resources management: recruitment and selection, remuneration; performance evaluation; career and promotion; training; conflict of interest; labour relations; and the termination of service.

The 2011 Act continues the previous practice of HRM decisions being highly decentralised, giving lots of power to the employer. For example, recruitment decisions are left to the employer including determining the recruitment procedure. Who is considered to be the employer depends on the type of government organisation. In the case of ministries the minister is the head of the organisation, but the employer's rights are delegated to the State secretary for administrative affairs. On the other hand, in case of central offices and the capital and county government offices the head of the organisation exercises the employer's rights.

The law does not require that vacant positions be openly advertised nor is there a requirement for a competitive selection procedure. It sets up some general requirements – such as nationality, clean police record, and legal capacity – and educational requirements.

The remuneration of civil servants consists of a base salary, which depends on their level of education and seniority, and is calculated according to pay tables included in the Act. Movement within a given salary grade is based on seniority. There is a salary supplement based on the type of agency the civil servant works for, which could reach 15-50% of the base salary. Special allowances also exist for having specific skills or working in dangerous or hazardous conditions, as well as anniversary bonuses and discretionary premiums. There is also another form of performance-related pay – beside premiums –, whereby the base salary of the civil servant can be increased by 50% or decreased by 20% based on the results of the performance appraisal. This amount does not build into the base salary and applies only for one year. Performance pay is determined by the employer.

For clerical staff (administrators) the salary table has been abolished and their salary is determined by the employer within the limits of the statutory minimum wage and six times the civil services salary base. For managerial positions remuneration is based solely on the level of responsibility and it does not reflect seniority. The lowest managerial wage is significantly higher than the highest possible non-managerial civil service wage.

Promotion to managerial position is also the prerogative of the employer as competitive selection is not compulsory. Based on the Act (par. 45. Sec. 1) appointments can happen on the basis of restricted or competitive procedure based on the law or the decision of the certain State administrative organ. But even in this case it is mandatory to apply the rules and standards of competitive procedure specified by law. However, there is no evidence whether these rules are implemented in the case of restricted procedures.

A career system element of the Hungarian civil service is the requirement to pass the basic civil service exam within the first two years of service and the advanced exam in order to be promoted into an advisor or managerial position. The new National University of Public Service is generally responsible for training and retraining of civil servants. Taking part in training is the right and duty of civil servants. According to Decree 273/2012 (IX.28) and the Act on Public Officials (kttv.), civil servants are obliged to participate in training annually.

Conflict of interest situations are legally determined and include economic, political, professional and personal types.

The 2011 Act established the new Chamber of "cabinet civil servants". It is a self-governing professional body in which membership for tenured government officials is mandatory. The main tasks of the Chamber are interest advocacy of government officials, participation in the codification of legal norms for the Cabinet civil service and the preparation of a code of ethics. There is also tripartite labour consultation where trade unions and representatives of associations of local governments participate besides the Government. Labour disputes go in first instance to a newly established Arbitration Board for cabinet civil servants, and on appeal to the Court.

According to the Civil Service Act the appointment of the civil servant is for an indefinite period, however, it can be terminated for many reasons defined by the Act. Civil servants could be laid off in case of termination of activity, termination of the organisation or its unit where the civil servant worked, reorganisation, downsizing, incapability of service or as a consequence of disciplinary procedure. Since 2010 two new reasons for dismissal have been introduced: behaviour that is incompatible with civil service status and the loss of the superior's confidence. According to the Government these two new reasons for termination have been added in order to strengthen the professional values of the civil service.

Civil servants are generally entitled to two months' notice. If a civil servant is dismissed by government for reasons not in the liability of the civil servant – e.g. restructuring – he/she is entitled to severance pay that depends on the length of service at the given office and it varies between one to eight months' salary.

Other elements of HRM reforms carried out during 2010-2013 as part of the Magyary Programmes included the piloting of a new job evaluation system, the introduction of a standardised performance evaluation system across the civil service and the development of the ethics code. The Magyary Programme had a strong focus on the improvement of integrity in the civil service from which one of the key achievements has been the creation of a network of integrity officers. Several staff engagement surveys have also been carried out during this period.

From 2010 to mid-2014 the Ministry of Public Administration and Justice was responsible for the civil service. After the 2014 elections this responsibility has been divided between the Prime Minister's Office that is responsible for setting strategic frameworks and policy directions for the whole government, including the civil service; the Ministry of Interior, that has responsibility for the implementation of the strategy, including digital government and HRM for the civil service and for municipalities.

What have been the key achievements in HRM from 2010-2014 and where is there a need for improvement?

Merit-based, neutral, professional civil service

The basic tenet of a good public administration is a merit-based, politically neutral, professional civil service motivated to perform to the best of its abilities to achieve the political goals of the elected officials. Our analysis of the existing HRM practices in the Hungarian civil service – and later the future reform plans – is based on evaluating how they contribute to the achievement of that. In addition, we examine whether the past and future reforms in the HRM area would be able to address the challenges the Hungarian government faces on the human resources front.

The vision of the PAPSDS talks about professional, highly qualified, ethical and motivated workforce with a national calling. The Magyary Programme, the Civil Service Act and the Government Staff Strategy together constitute the basis of the new public service career model programme, which set the reform directions for civil servants, law enforcement and defence staff.

The 2011 Act continues – similarly to the previous system – the highly delegated HRM system for the government officials with broad-ranging powers granted to the employer. Those powers encompass the recruitment and selection process, setting of performance pay, promotion decisions, as well as dismissal. In many OECD member countries with strong position-based systems line ministries/agencies have some or all of these decision-making powers as well. The key motive behind delegation is to empower and enable public managers to better direct their staff allowing them to consider both the unique requirements of their organisation and the merits of individual employees.

At the same time, delegation of HRM functions requires well-trained managers and some mechanisms to ensure standardisation of practices and their results among different units.

This is how delegation is carried out in many OECD countries that have delegated lots of decision-making power related to HRM practices to line departments and agencies, such as Sweden, Australia, and New Zealand. However, in those countries there are either legislated standards or central HRM policies and standards that managers have to follow that ensure consistent application of transparent merit principles. In many countries civil servants also belong to unions, that are representing the collective interest of civil servants and providing due processes for individual workers in case of arbitrary decisions made by managers. In Hungary civil service unions are relatively weak and are not fully able to fulfil these roles adequately. The Trade Union of Hungarian Civil Servants and Public Employees (MKKSZ) is the trade union for employees of State administrative organs, local governments, budgetary institutions, and economic and social organisations. Approximately 10-15% of the civil servants are members of trade unions. (source: Hungarian Ministry of Interior).

Box 3.1. Merit-based recruitment in the Australian public service

Employment decisions in the Australian Public Service (APS) are based on merit, which is one of the APS Values.

At a minimum, all employment decisions should be based on an assessment of a person's work-related qualities and those required to do the job. For decisions that may result in the engagement or promotion of an APS employee, the assessment must be competitive. Under the Public Service Act 1999, a decision is based on merit if:

- an assessment is made of the relative suitability of the candidates for the duties, using a competitive selection process; and

- the assessment is based on the relationship between the candidates' work-related qualities and the work-related qualities genuinely required for the duties; and

---

Box 3.1. Merit-based recruitment in the Australian public service *(continued)*

- the assessment focuses on the relative capacity of the candidates to achieve outcomes related to the duties; and

- the assessment is the primary consideration in making the decision.

For the assessment to be competitive, it should also be open to all eligible members of the community. For ongoing jobs and non-ongoing jobs for more than 12 months, this is achieved by notifying the job in the APS Employment Gazette on the APS jobs website.

Work-related qualities that may be taken into account when making an assessment include:

- Skills and abilities

- Qualifications, training and competencies

- Standard of work performance

- Capacity to produce outcomes from effective performance at the level required

- Relevant personal qualities

- Demonstrated potential for further development

- Ability to contribute to team performance.

Source: Information provided by the Australian Public Service Commission (via Colombia PGR).

In terms of central HRM policies regarding the recruitment and selection process, the most important standard practices are the open advertisement of positions and the competitive recruitment procedures that managers need to follow. These processes are fundamental to merit-based recruitment in order to avoid nepotism where recruitment and selection is based on personal loyalty. As a result, it is of utmost importance that these be established in Hungary as well.

Recommendation: *The role of competitive and standardised selection procedures need to be strengthened in civil servant recruitment. Effective mechanisms need to be developed to monitor that in the case of restricted recruitment the rules and standards of competitive procedure are applied.*

Recruitment without openness and merit-based requirements may undermine the neutrality of the civil service as well. In an ideal environment it is also the bureaucrats' role "to speak truth to power". This is usually achieved by a clear division of labour between, on the one hand, the politicians and their political staff and, on the other hand, the bureaucrats. The policy direction is set by the politicians, while its implementation is carried out by the bureaucracy. However, in that process bureaucrats need to be able to freely provide advice to their political masters not only about the benefits but also the potential shortcomings or unexpected consequences of their policy choices. Their advice should come from a politically neutral position.

The ability of providing politically neutral advice is considerably weakened by the termination section of the Civil Service Act, where one possible cause for termination is the loss of the superior's confidence. This might put civil servants to an untenable position of not being able to freely provide advice to their superiors.

According to the Act loss of confidence occurs when a civil servant does not fulfil his/her obligation – according to section 2 of paragraph 76 – with professional loyalty towards their manager. Professional loyalty should be understood as commitment towards the professional values defined by the manager, co-operation with the manager and colleagues and orderly and thorough task performance based on professional commitment. The cause of confidence loss can be, therefore, exclusively a piece of proved evidence concerning behaviour and task performance of the civil servant. However, if that is the case then termination for just cause can clearly be established and there would be no need for this special provision; creating uncertainty and instability that could result in high turnover.

According to the results of the Strategic HRM survey of the OECD (Government at a Glance, OECD, 2011) even before the enactment of the new Civil Service Act in 2011 in Hungary with a change of government up to 5 levels of management have been replaced, one of the highest number – besides Turkey – among OECD countries (OECD, 2011, Indicator 18.1). Large-scale turnover in managerial and also senior advisor positions do not only happen when government changes, but also with changes of the minister. For example, administrative State secretaries, professional heads and career civil servants in the Hungarian civil service spent on average 553 days in office, which is roughly identical to the period in office for the ministers – 517 days, and less in case of political secretaries; 560 days for ministers (Vanyi, 2013)[1]. This shows that not only political, but personal loyalty is expected from Hungarian civil servants. High turnover of civil servants counteracts the intentions of the Government to build a public service career model and sends wrong signals to potential recruits.

Recommendation: *HRM rules need to be strengthened to avoid subjective evaluation and decision-making by managers as a valid cause for termination of civil servants.*

Civil servant dissatisfaction with pay and benefits

Pay should reflect the skills/knowledge, effort, and responsibilities of the individual as well as special working conditions in order to motivate people to do their best. It also has to be considered fair both in the procedural sense – e.g. how it is set – and in its outcomes, both in absolute pay levels and in pay relativities.

According to the results of the employee engagement surveys conducted during 2010-2013 civil servants are highly unsatisfied with their pay and benefits.

---

[1] Vanyi, Eva (2013) A magyar kormanyzati elit 1990-2010 kozott. PhD thesis, Corvinus University of Budapest, 2013. Link: http://phd.lib.uni-corvinus.hu/721/1/Vanyi_Eva.pdf p.175.

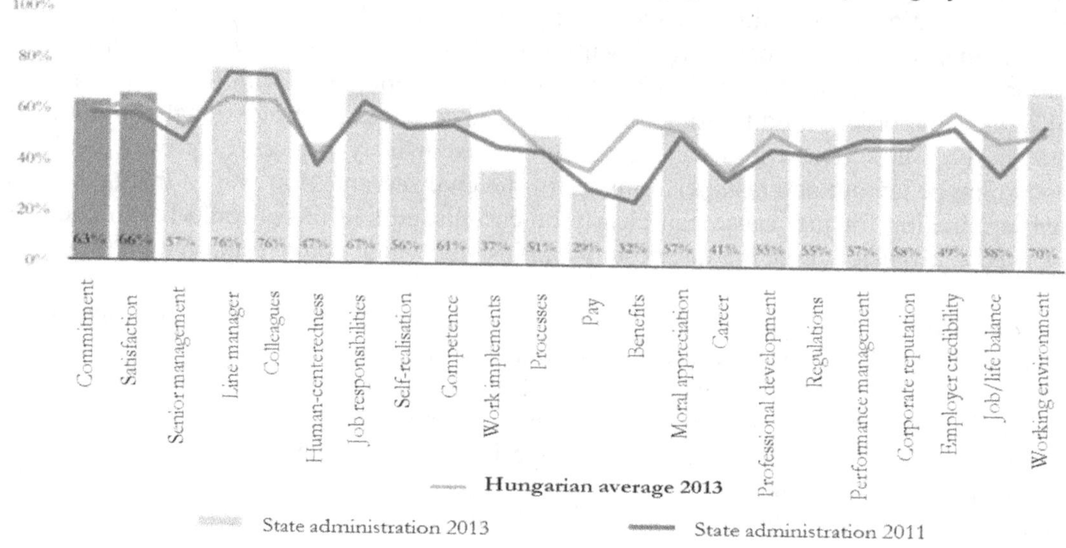

Figure 3.1. Results from the public servants engagement survey Hungary

Source: SROP 2.2.17 „New public service career" – Rate of public servant (government servant) commitment 2013. – Summary analysis.

Description of the columns: Commitment Satisfaction Senior management Line manager Colleagues Human-centredness Job responsibilities Self-realisation Competence Work implements Processes Pay Benefits Moral appreciation Career Professional development Regulations Performance management Corporate reputation Employer credibility Job/life balance Working environment

Source: Hungary Public Administration and Public Service Development Strategy 2014-2020.

Civil servants in Hungary are paid below the OECD average (OECD, 2011). The figures below show compensation levels and structures of middle managers and economist/policy analysts across OECD member countries in 2010. Their relative position compared to other OECD countries is worst for economist/policy analysts than for middle managers.

Adjusted for differences in working hours and holidays

Figure 3.2. Average annual compensation of middle managers in central government

Adjusted for differences in working hours and holidays

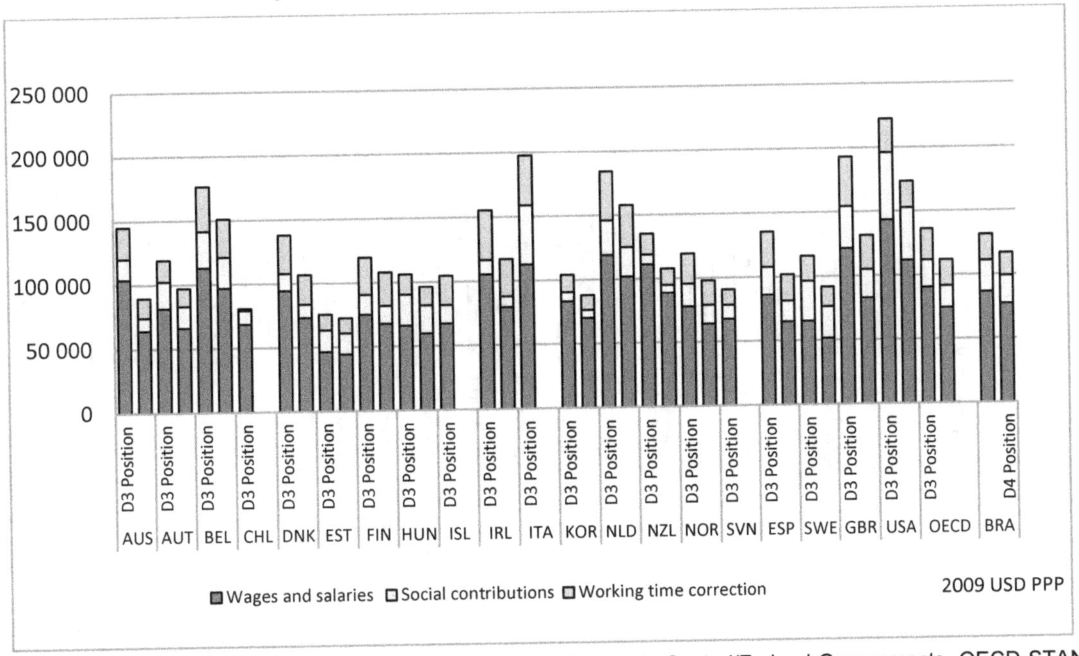

Source: 2010 OECD Survey on the Compensation of Employees in Central/Federal Governments, OECD STAN Database.

In terms of pay relativities, the difference between the highest paid (D1 - senior managers) and the lowest paid occupations (secretaries) is 4.8 in Hungary, while the ratio in the OECD is 4.5 (OECD, 2011). In terms of compensation structure, the ratio of social contributions paid by the employer is equal to 36.7% of the gross salary for all occupations (against 23.0% on average in OECD countries).

In the Hungarian civil service the base salary – which is usually the most important and largest part of remuneration in other OECD countries – is set artificially low and represents a relatively small percentage of overall pay. It is based on education levels and seniority, and, as a result, it is de-coupled from the actual tasks and efforts of the person, except for differentiating between analyst/advisor and managerial jobs, which reflects differences in responsibility. Actual tasks and performance are reflected in the many add-ons/supplements to the base pay that makes pay flexible and reflect special circumstances.

Many add-ons have been created presumably to counteract the shortcomings of the currently used base pay setting mechanism. At the same time, there are supplements which are hard to justify, such as the supplement based on the ministry/agency/municipality the person works for, that ranges between 15-50% of the base salary and it is a fixed portion of it. Seldom is this an explicit wage defining characteristic in other OECD countries. However, for example in New Zealand which has a very highly decentralised HRM system for civil servants, where even base wage-setting is decentralised, differences can be observed in how much civil servants are paid in the same position with similar seniority at different ministries or agencies (Lonti–Feinberg-Danieli, 2006).

Figure 3.3. Average annual compensation of economists and statisticians in central government

Adjusted for differences in working hours and holidays

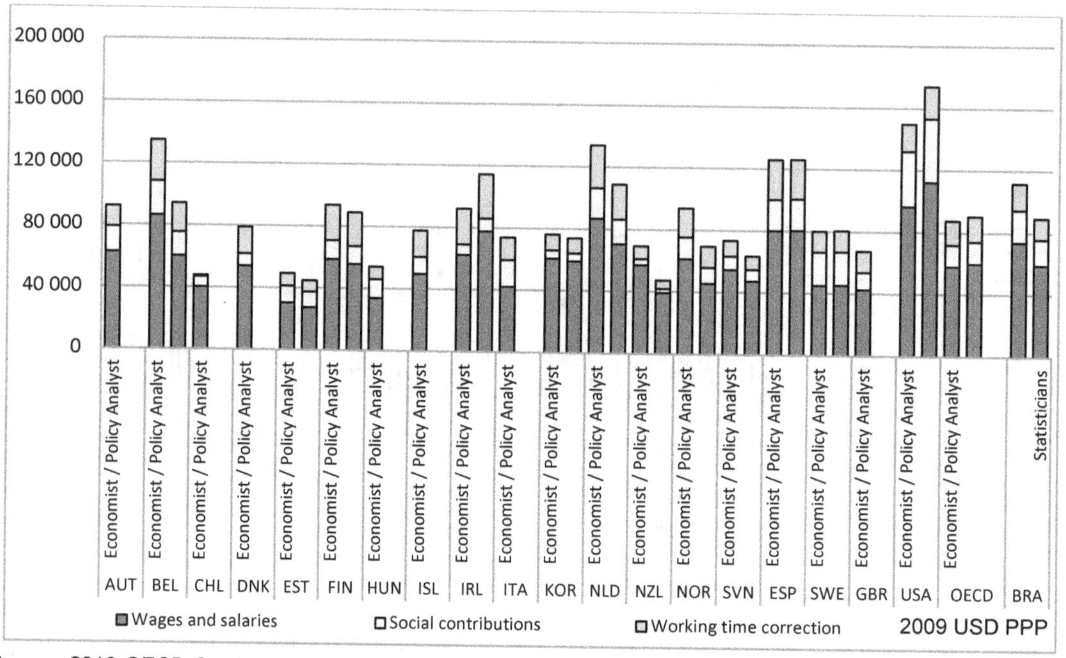

Source: 2010 OECD Survey on the Compensation of Employees in Central/Federal Governments, OECD STAN Database.

Performance pay could be a relatively large component of civil servants' pay which is dependent on the results of their performance evaluation. However, this brings a large element of subjectivity to the pay of the civil servants, as their performance is evaluated by their superiors and while it should be based on objective criteria, subjectivity would be very hard to avoid. This is not unique to Hungary, what is special in this case is that such a large part of the pay is dependent on it.

Regarding the evaluation of the civil servants, two types of evaluations are carried out in Hungary. One is called personal appraisal which focuses primarily on the competencies of the individual and to some degree also his/her performance and is used for the identification of skills gaps and also for promotion purposes. This has been a constant feature of the Hungarian civil service. To this has been added since 2002 – on and off – the annual performance evaluation system that could also be linked to performance pay and, in case of non-performance, could also be a reason for dismissal.

Carrying out performance evaluations became compulsory in 2013 and the same system applies to the public service, the police and the military. It has been introduced by government decrees 10/2013 (I.21) Gov. Decree on individual performance evaluation in the public service and 10/2013 (VI.30) Decree of the Ministry of Public Administration and Justice on the individual performance evaluation of public officials, and there is standardised software that line managers are required to use. It could be adapted to various organisations (e.g. ministries or municipalities) and contains several modules, including compulsory and suggested parts, individual and strategic competencies. It creates the possibility of 180 or 360 degrees evaluations. Standardisation of evaluation results are helped by behavioural scales containing examples of concrete behaviours. Competencies can be tailored to the individual and linked to job descriptions. The introduction of the system has been accompanied by the training of 4,000 staff – HRM people and managers – in the methodology, who act as support and resource persons. Currently bonuses for extraordinary performance are linked to the results of performance evaluations as well as the awarding of salary increments (between +50% and -20% of the base pay). Awarding bonuses instead of raising base pay is a cost-effective way for employers to reward good performance of individuals.

Figure 3.4. Extent of the use of performance assessments in HR decisions in central government (2010)

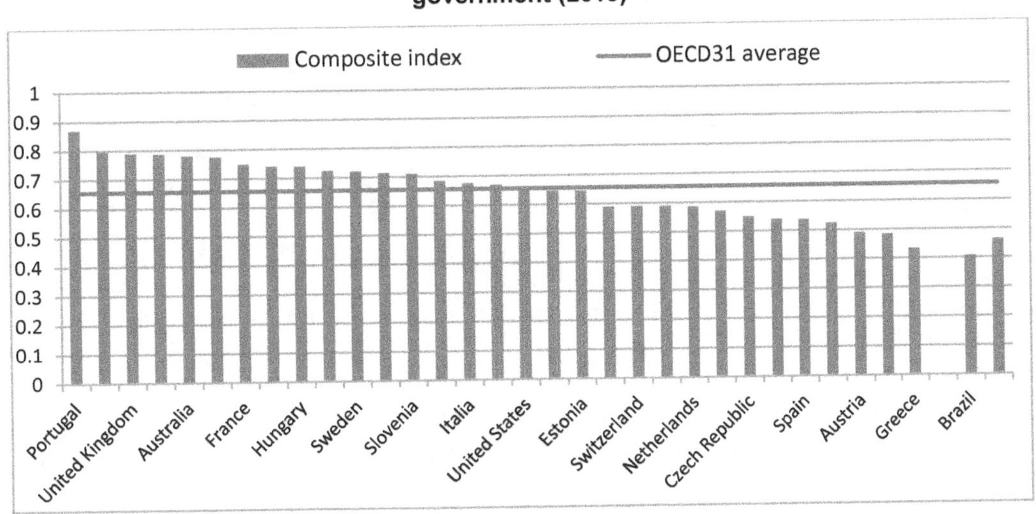

Source: 2010 OECD Survey on Strategic Human Resources Management in Central/Federal Governments (published in Government at a Glance 2011).

There has been increased emphasis on performance pay in many OECD countries (Government at a Glance 2011, OECD). However, there is no consensus in the literature or among practitioners regarding how it effects the motivation of civil servants and whether it is successful in increasing their performance (OECD, 2012). There are several problem areas in applying performance pay for civil service jobs. First of all, the type of performance pay that is used in government is usually individualised, while the tasks carried out by civil servants are most of the time highly interdependent. Secondly, it is hard – or almost impossible – to measure the actual performance of individuals in many of the civil service jobs. In the absence of measurable outputs or outcomes, and faced with serious attribution problems, performance pay in the civil service is often linked to individual performance evaluations carried out by line managers. However, with those performance evaluations the subjective judgment of the line manager is introduced into the system. There is a vast literature on what are the errors that managers are prone to commit in the evaluation process. As a result, standardisation of the appraisal process and training line managers on how to properly conduct performance evaluations is critical to its successful application. As part of the Magyary Programme a standardised performance evaluation system has been introduced to the whole civil service. This is an important step of making the process more credible.

Figure 3.5. Extent of the use of performance-related pay in central government (2010)

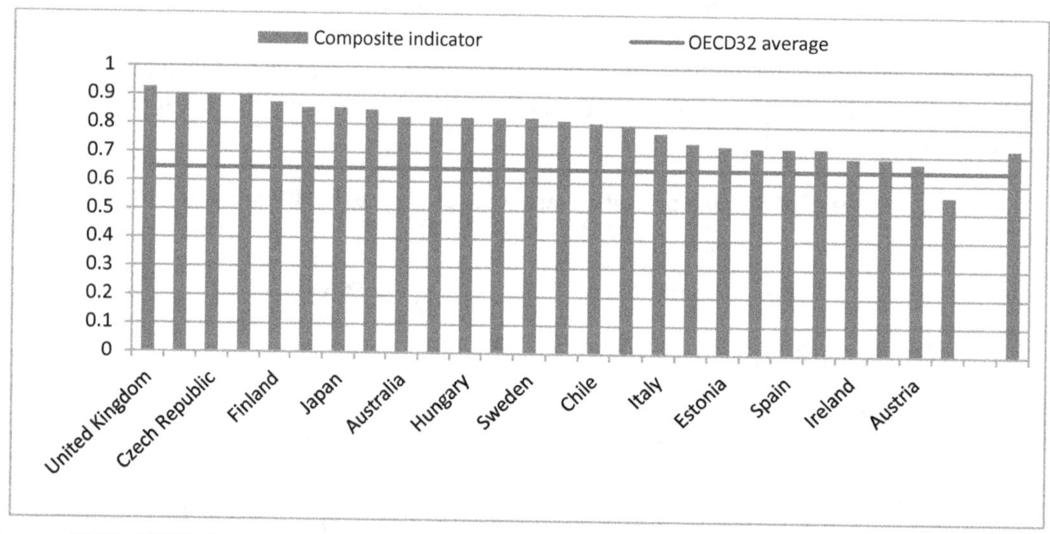

Source: 2010 OECD Survey on Strategic Human Resources Management in Central/Federal Governments (published in Government at a Glance 2011).

In order to create a consistent, coherent system of HRM practices and also address civil servants' dissatisfaction with their pay, besides raising salary levels there is also a need to redesign the pay system. Seniority is used less and less as a determinant of base salary in civil service jobs, several OECD countries are moving away from automatic pay increases based on seniority. Movement in the salary grade is linked to the results of performance evaluations, such as in the NZ civil service. Pay systems are built focusing less on the characteristics of the individual and more on the characteristics of the job that the individual occupies. In that case job evaluation plays a key role, creating systematically a hierarchy of jobs to which pay can be linked. A rigorous job evaluation system also introduces procedural fairness into wage-setting, thereby increasing the overall fairness of the resulting wage system as well. A well-designed and -executed job evaluation system also allows identifying the key competencies for the various job families and can be used as a basis for training needs assessment, and as a useful tool to build career paths.

Box 3.2. United Kingdom: Lessons from experience with performance-related pay (Hutton Review)

The Hutton Review of Fair Pay in the Public Sector was commissioned in 2010 by the Prime Minister and the Chancellor of the Exchequer with the objective of ensuring fairness in public sector pay in the context of current economic circumstances. Findings in relation to the use of performance-related pay included:

- Performance is better measured in terms of outcomes over time rather than against peers, whether at the level of organisations or individuals.

  Strictly quantifiable measures can have pitfalls, especially when used to rank individuals and organisations in great detail. The choice of performance measures can affect the results. However, objective measures can be a powerful way of driving a conversation in which staff members have to account for their performance. More finely tuned judgemental assessments can include 360-degree and stakeholder reviews. Where necessary, there should be a move away from specific targets to the

---

Box 3.2. United Kingdom: Lessons from experience with performance-related pay (Hutton Review) *(continued)*

use of more general success criteria, such as benchmarks and milestones, which are harder to manipulate.

- Performance appraisal is the backbone of the whole system, without which pay decisions become arbitrary. A high priority should be attached to consultation with employees as well as to simple and regular communication, so that different goals are recognised and objectives are transparent.

- Where feasible, performance indicators should be based on alternative, independent and manipulation–proof information sources. The distribution of rewards should be controlled and co-ordinated by independent committees. These tasks have been made easier by advances in technology that allow for the rapid collection and processing of information.

- Rating systems should avoid forced rankings as this can create divisiveness among employees. If it is necessary to use ranking systems, they should be used more to check the distribution than as a rigid quota.

- Objectives should be relatively stable over time and to the extent possible should be protected from political interference. Performance assessments should involve defining medium-term measures of success and placing considerable weight on them. In part this can be done by requiring that the choice of short-term performance measures correlate empirically and theoretically with positive long-term outcomes.

Source: United Kingdom Government (2011), *Hutton Review of Fair Pay in the Public Sector*, HM Treasury, webarchive.nationalarchives.gov.uk/20130129110402, www.hmtreasury.gov.uk/indreview_willhutton_easyread.htm

As part of the Magyary Programme the Hay system, a prominent job evaluation system has been piloted in 2012 for 1,000 jobs, and was scaled up in 2013. Jobs are evaluated based on the skills/knowledge required to carry them out, the need for problem-solving, responsibility, and working conditions. The system has been applied not only to government officials' jobs, but also to police, military and disaster recovery jobs (Hungarian Presentation, September, 2014).

Recommendation: *The Strategy should also include the redesign of the civil service pay system, to link it more to the requirements of the jobs using the results of job evaluation and rethink performance pay in a way that increases civil servants' motivation and performance.*

From this evaluation, it is clear that the introduction of the new job evaluation system and the standardised performance evaluation system are successful achievements of the Magyary Programmes, together with the creation of the National Public Service University that has been instrumental is providing the necessary training that needed to accompany the major organisational and work design changes at both the central and territorial public administration. At the university the training of civil servants, policy and military personnel happens together and side-by-side, creating the first necessary step to the public service career model. The university is also leading the research that underpins the public sector reform programme. Another achievement on the training front is the establishment and continued fine-tuning of the central electronic portal ProBono, which provides many types of courses/training to both public servants and managers in the form of e-learning and blended learning courses.

The prevention of corruption is a top priority also in Hungary, and therefore an integrity management system was introduced in 2013 for the management of corruption risks within the organisations concerned, combined with extensive managerial and government servant training.

By considering these recommendations to making changes to selected HRM practices attraction of the Hungarian civil service might be improved and turnover – which is relatively high – might be reduced, and a more motivated and engaged workforce can be achieved.

What are the HRM reform components of the PAPSDS 2014-2020?

This section describes the key HRM reform components of the PAPSDS 2014-2020. The key challenges identified regarding human resources by the Hungarian government are difficulties of attracting highly qualified professionals to the public service, as well as with retention of well-performing staff. Implicitly there is also the assumption that there is a need to improve the overall performance of staff. The solution offered is the creation of a strategic, integrated competency-based human resources management system to serve the establishment of a public service career model. It also includes corresponding HRM reforms at local governments, which is not addressed in this report.

The public service career model will not apply solely to the civil service, but also to law enforcement and the military. It will entail flexible transfers and mobility not just between the different positions within the various orders of professions – civil service, law enforcement and the military – but also across them. In order to accomplish that, there is a need for an integrated regulatory background of HRM policies and practices that applies to all three orders of professions.

The cornerstone of the career model is a well-designed job evaluation system. A common job evaluation system applicable to all three orders of professions will be implemented. The system has been successfully applied already to 15,000 jobs as part of the Magyary Programmes, covering both civil service and law enforcement jobs. Job evaluation is key, as it forms the basis of job descriptions, helps identify the competency requirements of jobs; could be used for the creation of job families and career paths, the creation and maintenance of conditions of promotion and flexible transfers, as well as for the development of modular training system adjusted to the competency requirements of jobs. It also allows the transformation of the remuneration system – which is part of the planned HRM reforms – based on the relative value of jobs, thereby enhancing the competitiveness of the public service in the labour market. It could also be used to identify risks of corruption for individual jobs.

The career model will be built upon a competency-based human resources management system. Between 2014 and 2020, general competency development – facilitating the personnel's horizontal movement – will be the main priority for the Hungarian public service, as entry into the public service career, performance- and knowledge-based promotion, job-based management and flexible transfers within public service require the complex and ongoing development of staff. This requires the reform of the system of qualification requirements accompanied by a corresponding modular competency development training system.

Competency development cannot be carried out without ongoing training for all three orders of professions, including systematic assessment of training needs based on performance evaluations and the set-up of individual development plans, and the development and implementation of differentiated training programmes. Planned training programmes are targeting a wide range of skills, including professional, technical, managerial, digital, and language skills.

The implementation of the strategy will require the strengthening of the HRM capacities of ministries and agencies, improving their professionalism, increasing their flexibility, as well as the establishment of better quality selection systems. Better selection procedures and further training of managers is necessary as well in order to develop a professional managerial culture.

Movement across jobs and across the orders of professions also need more flexible employment conditions which will be achieved by the institution of the public service contract. There will be specific rules applicable to the employment of senior members of staff.

The new public service career model aims to attract talent and reduce turnover by the development of attractive expert career paths, personalised career management, remuneration adjusted to the relative value of jobs and to performance, and various scholarship programmes. In conjunction with the performance evaluation process, there is a need for developing a talent management system for motivated staff members with outstanding performance. It is necessary to co-ordinate the talent management system with the expert career model to ensure that the benefits of sharing outstanding individual skills, abilities and good practices are enjoyed at the staff member's place of work and contribute to organisational developments, thereby improving organisational performance. Performance evaluations need to be linked to personnel development, incentives and career management.

Enhancing the commitment of staff members also helps retain them in public administration. This may be achieved primarily through the recognition of performance and knowledge, the wider involvement of staff members, and the improvement of working conditions. Public service career satisfaction may also be improved by welfare, social and other services which are designed to help resolve the specific problems that may emerge during certain career stages.

Increased involvement of staff members, which simultaneously boosts the self-corrective capability of public administration, may be used as a means for motivation. The increased involvement of the personnel in the formulation of developments concerning work processes and professional issues also means the recognition of their professional expertise, and additionally promotes their identification with the organisational goals.

New welfare, social and other service provider activities will be carried out by the Corps by creating a separate public service life and accident insurance scheme and reinforcing the supplementary pension and health insurance system that has operated well since 1993. A comprehensive survey of living and housing conditions and state of health of staff will be carried out in order to introduce services that satisfy actual needs. A public service employer pension scheme and an integrated public service holiday scheme are planned as well. The employment of people with special needs will also be promoted (e.g. young mothers, handicapped people).

A career model cannot function without up-to-date information on the characteristics of personnel. To achieve that, Hungary is committed to the creation of a core public service registration system as well as a standard personnel and monitoring system.

Further development of the integrity management system established by the Magyary Programmes is targeted as well. The current system primarily focuses on organisational integrity. In the future it will be harmonised with the internal controlling system, the quality management system and the executive information system. Job evaluation will allow assessing of corruption risks of the individual jobs and will allow adopting targeted preventive measures.

Analysis of the planned HRM reforms for 2014-2020

Strategic human resource management aligns HRM practices to the strategic goals of government. It allows governments to have the right number of people in the right place with the right competencies. It also requires that there should be consistency of HRM practices with the broader State reform strategy (vertical fit), as well as consistency among the HRM practices (horizontal fit). In our evaluation of the planned HRM reforms we focus on whether these vertical and horizontal consistencies could be achieved. We also evaluate whether the proposed reforms will make the public service more attractive, allow for increased retention of well-performing staff and will create proper incentives to increase staff performance that could translate into better governmental performance.

The utilisation of strategic human resources management practices has been operationalised by the OECD (OECD, 2011) by a composite indicator that looks at the extent to which centralised HRM bodies use a general accountability framework for top managers; whether HRM targets are built into the performance assessment of top and middle managers; the existence of regular reviews and assessment of HRM capacity of government organisations and other tools to engage in and promote strategic workforce planning. However, if these strategic HRM practices are delegated to the ministry/department/agency level they are not reflected in this index. In Hungary strategic HRM practices have been delegated to the ministry/agency level, and as a result, in 2010 – the last time this information was collected – among OECD countries Hungary scored the lowest on this indicator. In section 4.3 we have described that HRM in Hungary is highly delegated, while the Magyary Programmes extensively focused on strategic planning issues. However, whether this also meant the inclusion of these strategic HRM practices into strategic planning is not clear. The new HRM reform plans do not mention these practices explicitly. However, an important part of the reforms are the set-up of a core public service registration system as well as a standard personnel and monitoring system, which could form the basis of workforce planning and the creation of the career model. But the use of other strategic tools in HRM need to be further strengthened.

Figure 3.6. Utilisation of strategic HRM practices in central government (2010)

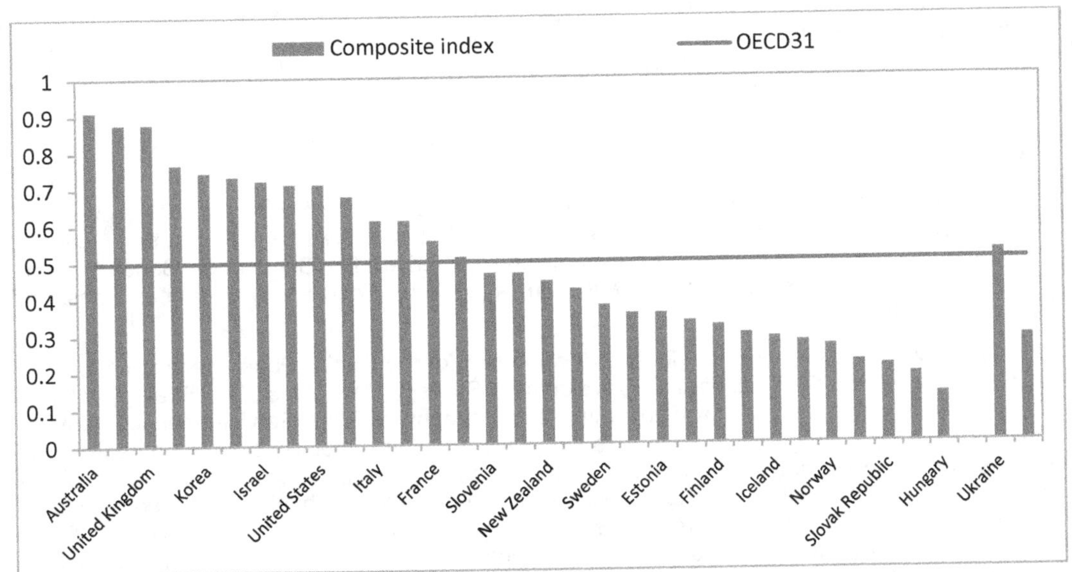

Source: 2010 OECD Survey on Strategic Human Resources Management in Central/Federal Governments (published in Government at a Glance 2011).

Recommendation: *There is a need to strengthen strategic HRM focusing on better workforce planning and reviews and assessments of HRM capacities of organisations. This could be carried out as part of increasing the HRM capabilities.*

As one of the key strategic HRM practices relate to how performance objectives for managers are linked to the strategic goals of government, which might be addressed under the special HRM practices that could be pursued for senior executives. This is mentioned – albeit very briefly – in the new HRM reforms.

Senior civil servants are located at a critical junction between strategy-making and strategy execution in government. Because of their strategic roles in government, there is an increased tendency among OECD countries – observed in 23 OECD countries in 2010 – to group senior civil servants separately and manage them under different HRM policies. They tend to be recruited by a more centralised process and there is a defined skill/competency profile applied to them specifically. In this group greater emphasis is placed on capacity-building and on incentivising improved performance through higher portion of their remuneration being performance-related. In some countries potential leadership is systematically identified either at entry or early in their careers, and staff careers are managed accordingly. This did not exist in 2010 and does not exist currently in the Hungarian government.

Box 3.3. Setting up a Senior Public Service in Ireland

The current Programme for Government contains a commitment to "create a new tier of senior public service management structures to nurture the collaborative culture needed to tackle the biggest cross-cutting social and economic challenges". The establishment of the Senior Public Service provides an opportunity to develop a shared public sector leadership and corporate resource which is consolidated by common public service values and experiences, but which also challenges established mindsets and culture and seeks to adapt in the face of new norms, risks and challenges.

The vision for the SPS is:

To build a community of leaders that supports national recovery and builds renewal through innovation and excellence, strengthening cross-organisational collaboration, supporting continuous personal and professional development and inspiring others to achieve high performance in a common purpose.

Membership of the Senior Public Service currently comprises civil servants at Director level and above. The total current SPS membership is around 240.

The SPS Management Committee, which was established in December 2011, oversees policy in relation to developmental initiatives for the SPS. It is chaired by the Secretary General, Department of Public Expenditure and Reform and comprises the Secretaries General of the Departments of the Taoiseach; Social Protection; Agriculture, Food and the Marine; Transport, Tourisms and Sport; and Defence.

The key aims and processes for the development of the Senior Public Service cohort are set out in the current SPS Leadership Development Strategy 2013-2015. The Strategy reflects the need to support the 'whole-of-government' philosophy of Civil Service management by supporting the top management cohort as a single resource, with mobility between organisations and a structured development programme for the members of the Service. The goal is to equip the SPS with the skills and supports necessary on meeting the key business challenges facing the Civil Service. It also aims to create a shared sense of purpose and focus in meeting these challenges. The key learning and development components of the Strategy which are currently in train are the SPS Executive Coaching Programme, senior level mobility and the holding of regular networking events. Further learning and development opportunities for SPS members will come on stream as these programmes are embedded.

Source: Provided to the OECD by the Irish Peer.

Recommendation: *Consider creating a separate senior civil service with special HRM practices that will help closer align their behaviours and performance to the Government's objectives.*

There are two distinctive features of the planned HRM reforms in Hungary from 2014-2020 (1) the creation of a joint HRM system as a prerequisite for increased mobility not just inside civil service, law enforcement and the military but also among them; and (2) the selection of a career model of HRM in order to improve attraction and retention of the public service.

The HRM reforms proposed such as the common public service contract, joint job evaluation system, joint performance management system, changes to the prerequisite qualifications, the emphasis on competencies and the introduction of modular competency development training systems are complementary to each other and form an integrated system of leading-edge HRM practices all serving the objective of increased flexibility and mobility across the three orders of professions.

Box 3.4. Competency Management in the Belgian Federal Government

In the Belgian public services – both federal and regional – competencies are at the core of every HRM process, be it recruiting and selecting, career management, performance appraisal and 360-degree feedback, knowledge management or the identification of critical functions. The greatest advantage of this approach is that competencies are linked to organisational needs – tactical or strategic – and that they provide a common language for all parties across the different services.

Competency management has been a central element since the launch of the Copernic Plan in 2000, focusing on a more integrated and strategic approach to HRM. It fundamentally

---

Box 3.4. Competency Management in the Belgian Federal Government *(continued)*

changed recruitment and selection procedures, training and development, introducing workforce planning linked to organisational objectives.

The competency framework consists of:

- Five key competencies that reflect the values of the federal government: service delivery orientation, team co-operation, loyalty, result orientation and self-development

- Five groups of generic competencies considered necessary for all functions: information management; task management; management of employees; management of relationships; and personal management

- A large group of technical competencies which are specific to a type of work and supporting the profession itself.

A competency dictionary is available as a tool for HRM services, managers, chefs and employees. There are 22 standard competency profiles, built around 3 roles: support, management and project management adapted to the employee level.

Implementing competency management resulted in some major recruitment system changes. The emphasis in entrance examinations shifted from testing knowledge to testing competencies. New procedures were put in place using a professional recruitment agency. Line managers and local HRM services are responsible for providing a job description and a competency profile for every recruitee (online standard profiles: www.federalecartografie.be/web/p1.php?z=z&lg=fr).

Providing a comprehensive and clear-cut framework for managers is an ongoing priority in which the appropriate competencies play a key role as they determine the profile and remuneration of a manager. The framework depends on 12 generic competencies to which competencies specific to the position can be added. The competencies are:

- Thinking (analysis; flexibility and *innovation*; vision and capacity for integration)

- Human resource management (coaching, motivation and development of personnel; team management)

- Interaction with the environment (collaboration and development of networks; orientation to citizens, internal clients and society)

- Objectives (sense of responsibility; achievement of objectives; persuasion and negotiation)

- Loyalty and integrity.

There is a strong link between competency management and performance appraisal as the annual evaluation scheme includes a discussion on the required competencies leading to (individual and team) development plans and training. Knowledge management is built around competencies, especially the technical competencies forming the heart of each function.

Source: OECD (2007b), *OECD Reviews of Human Resource Management in Government: Belgium*, OECD Publishing, Paris.

The increased flexibility and mobility among the three orders of professions is somewhat unique among OECD countries, although in the US federal government there is a strong push for hiring veterans. The Hungarian government argues that this mobility already exists and the new provisions just make it more transparent. According to their evaluation, there are many similarities between these three orders of professions, e.g. in their ethic and examination systems, trainings, career and remuneration systems as well as state care. Moreover, all the three orders of professions have the characteristic of exercising public authority, regulated activity and hierarchical structure. However, the police and the army are organised around a more command and control type of management which fits their task specificities. This might not be applicable to the same extent to public administration that have to find innovative solutions to complicated, wicked problems which require a more dispersed and collaborative type of leadership. As a result, in most OECD countries these three orders of professions have separate career tracks. Most of the suggested HRM reforms – the full implementation of the job evaluation system, the competency-focused HRM practices, the development of clear career paths, the provision of a competency-based training system and the many training opportunities – help create a career model of civil/public service. However, this career model has other important pre-requisites as well, namely strict merit-based recruitment and promotion processes including open advertisement of all positions and standardised competitive selection procedures. In addition, the removal of managerial subjectivity from termination provisions could also help persuade people that they indeed can have a long career in the civil service – or the broader public service –, longer than the tenure of their manager, their current minister or the government of the day. This has been discussed in detail under 4.3.

Other suggested reforms, such as further extension of standardised performance assessment procedures, changes to the remuneration system linking it to the relative value of the jobs as well as to performance are instrumental in improving both individual and organisational performance. Suggestions on how the remuneration system could be further developed are described in 4.3.

A new system of remuneration coupled with salary increases could also improve the attractiveness of the public service as well as employee retention. Increased employee participation and improved benefits – health, pension, and vacation – could also help achieve those objectives. These reforms also address the major areas of dissatisfaction identified by the staff engagement surveys related to pay, benefits and career opportunities. The creation of expert career path, personalised career management and talent management are also appropriate HRM management practices to attract the "best and the brightest", and to keep them.

The career model envisaged by the Hungarian government does not equate to the classical career-based model that has been the hallmark of HRM practices in government most closely associated with the Weberian state model. The current legislative environment for the civil service and the new HRM reforms create a mix between a career- and position-based system, becoming closer to a position-based one. The major characteristics of a career-based system is highly competitive merit-based recruitment at the start of their career, well-set-out pathways for career progression, lots of training opportunities, more emphasis on socialisation of new entrants to instil common, core public sector ethics and values and motivation as opposed to strong direct performance incentives; pay linked to both education levels, seniority and responsibility and last but not least, high job security. In a career-based system it is difficult to join the civil service mid-career from the outside. In a position-based system there is also merit-based competitive recruitment, but it is carried out for each position as opposed to at joining the civil service. Major differences to the career-based system are a stronger direct performance focus where pay is less linked to seniority and more to position, responsibility and performance and the use of more flexible employment contracts, and finally life-time tenure does not exist anymore.

Looking at the HRM system of the Hungarian civil service entry to it could happen any time. Passing the competitive examination is not a prerequisite for hiring and could be completed one year after starting the employment, with the exception of junior clerks, who have two years to do so. While base pay is currently based on education and seniority, performance pay is also playing an increasingly important role. While there are lots of training opportunities and the Government is working hard on establishing some clear career paths, the current system is much closer to a position-based one than to a career-based one. The introduction of job evaluation and linking it to pay also points to a movement more towards a position-based system. On the other hand, a well-executed job evaluation system introduces also more fairness – both in the procedural and outcome sense – into the HRM system.

Fighting corruption is still a major objective for the Hungarian public administration. The achievements regarding improved integrity practices are notable from 2010-2014 and the new plans in this regard are also promising. However, these reforms need to be rigorously evaluated not just by their outputs – e.g. how many integrity officer jobs have been created, how many integrity plans have been developed – but by trying to measure whether corruption – or citizens' and businesses' perception of corruption – has been declining.

Finally, the highly delegated system of HRM that is typical in Hungarian government and the new reforms require both strong central HRM policy directions as well as improved implementation capacity on the ground. It is not clear which organisation – the Prime Minister's Office or the Ministry of Interior – would be able to provide that central direction. As to the implementation of the reforms the planned increase of HRM capacities in ministries and agencies and better selection of managers and more managerial training might go a long way to facilitate those happening.

REFERENCES

Institute for Citizen-Centred Service (consulted on the 25th March, 2015: http://www.iccs-isac.org/en/about/service.htm).

Linder, Viktoria (2014) Balancing between Models: Job Security as a Determinant for Classification.

OECD (2007b), *OECD Reviews of Human Resource Management in Government: Belgium*, OECD Publishing, Paris.

OECD (2009), *Government at a Glance 2009 edition*. OECD Publishing, Paris. ISBN 978-92-64-0614-4

OECD (2010), *2010 OECD Survey on the Compensation of Employees in Central/Federal Governments*, OECD STAN Database.

OECD (2011), *2010 OECD Survey on Strategic Human Resources Management in Central/Federal Governments* (published in *Government at a Glance 2011*, OECD Publishing, Paris).

OECD (2011), *Government at a Glance 2011 edition*. OECD Publishing, Paris. http://dx.doi.org/10.1787/gov_glance-2011-en

OECD (2015a), *Hungary: Towards a Strategic State Approach*, OECD Public Governance Reviews, OECD Publishing. http://dx.doi.org/10.1787/9789264213555-en

OECD (2015b), *OECD Regulatory Policy Outlook 2015*, OECD Publishing, Paris. DOI: http://dx.doi.org/10.1787/9789264238770-en

"Merit-based recruitment in the Australian public service" – information provided by the Australian Public Service Commission (via Colombia Public Governance Review).

"Setting up a Senior Public Service in Ireland" – information provided by the Irish Peer.

SROP 2.2.17 *„New public service career" – Rate of public servant (government servant) commitment 2013. – Summary analysis*, in: Hungary Public Administration and Public Service Development Strategy 2014-2020.

"Vision for the Public Administration and Public Service Development Strategy of Hungary, 2014-2020" – information provided by the Prime Minister's Office of Hungary, 2015.

United Kingdom Government (2011), *Hutton Review of Fair Pay in the Public Sector*, HM Treasury, webarchive.nationalarchives.gov.uk/20130129110402, www.hmtreasury.gov.uk/indreview_willhutton_easyread.htm.

The Civil Services System in Hungary (2014) in Patyi, Andras and Rixer, Adam, Hungarian Public Administration and Administrative Law. pp. 501-520. Scherk Verlag.

The Hungarian Civil Service System in a European Comparative Context. Presented at the 22nd NISPAcee Annual Conference: XII. Working Group on Administration & Management of Internal Security Agencies. Budapest, Hungary, 2014.05.22-2014.05.24. Bratislava: NISPAcee, 2014. (ISBN: 978-80-89013-72-2).

Vanyi, Eva (2013) *A magyar kormanyzati elit* 1990-2010 kozott. PhD thesis, Corvinus University of Budapest, 2013. Link: http://phd.lib.uni-corvinus.hu/721/1/Vanyi_Eva.pdf

Chapter 4

Digital building blocks of a modern public administration in Hungary

Detailed evaluations of the current situation and the Hungarian government's digital strategy are included in this chapter which also answers key questions including: How far is Hungary from its vision of a digital state where government, citizens and businesses are taking full advantage of what digital technology offers? How does the government's strategy fit with the digital maturity of Hungarian society? How much is evidence used in making decisions? What are the pros and cons of the solutions selected for inter-operability and electronic identification? How much are governance options and leadership considered in achieving the desired outcomes?

Introduction

Hungary has invested remarkable efforts to define a digital component as part of its latest public administration modernisation strategy. The Public Administration and Public Service Development Strategy 2014-2020[1] together with the National Infocommunication Strategy 2014-2020 of Hungary is in fact paving the way for a digital government policy which meets the OECD definition of using "digital technologies as an integrated part of governments' modernisation strategies to create public value".

The Strategy has a digital component and defines a vision for a digital State which is one of the four pillars of the National Infocommunication Strategy 2014-2020. Through this "Digital State" vision[2] the Government aims to support an administrative reform with a focus on citizens' needs and it fosters the digital transformation of the public sector. The Strategy builds on achievements of the previous, so called Magyary Programmes and plans to go beyond the process of administrative simplification. Expected goals include improving the general business environment and boosting competitiveness; and digital services are seen as a key to delivering the expected results.

Nevertheless, there are a few success factors that we would recommend to the Hungarian government to consider in the context of the Public Service Development Strategy's plans as highlighted in this chapter.

Consider performing and presenting the definition of a vision and policy options on its implementation based on user take-up targets. Apply quantitative targets (e.g. certain percentage of 1-Population, 2-Internet users, 3-Client Gate registered users to use by specific dates digital services). Consider mandatory policy as an option for those who are ready by adopting a "stick and carrot" strategy for certain digital services and scaling them up while preventing digital exclusion.

Collecting and using evidence to ground policy options and broaden the digital State vision to boost competitiveness

Exploring links with existing practices

In the last years the Hungarian government has made efforts to define public administration modernisation priorities and implement a previously called Magyary Programme. The current, Public Service Development Strategy 2014-2020 (referred to as "Strategy") ensures business continuity and builds on the achievements such as those in administrative simplification. One of the concerns pointed out by the OECD in its 2014 report[3] was the lack of reference to digital government and its potential contribution to competitiveness and growth. This latest Strategy sets out a vision for "digitalisation". Namely, its strategic vision for a „good State" is planned to be achieved through a "Digital State" and digital government services. The "Digital State" is seen as a catalyst of a modernisation process.

This approach is in line with the OECD Council Recommendation on Digital Government Strategies noting[4] that "the challenge is not to introduce digital technologies into public administrations but to integrate their use into public sector modernisation efforts." Hungary is one of the countries which have started to shift from a technology-driven approach (e-Government) towards a how to use "digital solutions" for the benefits of public sector reforms. More information could be provided on which international examples have contributed to defining elements of the Strategy in response to a "digital challenge". There is a general need to build up a more informed digital vision and perform further harmonisation with the National Infocommunication Strategy 2014-2020 as time requires. Deeper integration possibilities between a "digital" vision and administrative reform could be considered.

Using data and evidence for strategic services and policies design

The Strategy covers objectives to build up a more effective, competitive and trusted public administration.

There are at least four dimensions that the Strategy would act upon:

1. Efficiency and effectiveness of public service delivery which lies in the heart of the Strategy and facilitated through internal process revision (e.g. administrative simplification and deregulation) accompanied with severe actions on quality assurance. These both refer to a more cost-efficient management of internal resources and to the focus on delivering better value for money to the customers: better quality at lower costs for all parties.

2. Competitiveness is treated in a broader sense and refers to both the optimal internal operation of the public administration and the high quality of services. Competitiveness is seen as being influenced by bureaucracy and government's capacity to offer business-favourable environments.

3. Building trust through a customer-focused approach is set in the centre of the Strategy. It refers to a commitment of the Government to develop a "service provider and people-oriented public sector".

4. Bringing public services close to the customers through a multichannel service delivery and digital solutions available 24/7.

The Strategy sets ambitious targets in cutting administration fees for customers and sets up controlling mechanisms for better decisions. On the other hand, the Strategy in its SWOT analysis refers to a threat of potential shifting in efforts from customers to the administration. In the absence of evidence and detailed analytical support the assessment of whether the goals and indicators are S.M.A.R.T.[5] cannot be performed. The Strategy provides limited information on how existing statistics and evidence are used to inform policy decisions and the whole implementation process. The Government could select and apply more evidence, various sources of statistical data and define S.M.A.R.T. goals during policy design.

Broadening perspective and reaping benefits building on general digital readiness

The scope of the Strategy is the public administration and that is reflected in the goal-setting and measures. Nevertheless, a comprehensive view on a broader digital maturity picture in the Hungarian society could inform policies. The whole digital government ecosystem and users of digital services of any kind can feed the decisions with statistics. The public sector reforms need to follow different approaches based on the target groups they are covering. Hungary is addressing the digital divide and implements initiatives such as "government windows" to be close to the citizens. In addition, there might be strengths such as a growing number of Internet or smartphone users which should not be overlooked.

Before implementing any solution, existing customers' habits and level of maturity, trust (e.g. certain percentage of potential users have smartphones or used e-payments in other contexts) needs to be analysed. One of the elements that digital strategies need to take into account is the relevance of the digital readiness of citizens. It can have a crucial role in taking up on digital public services.

For instance, in the last three years in Hungary, a stable Internet user group has been identified which counts up to 70-74% of the population[6]. In the same years about 70% of the households had broadband connection.[7] According to the most recent DESI – Digital Economy & Society Index[8] of the European Commission – Hungary ranks 20th out of the 28 Member States. This study confirms that Hungary in 2014 has been catching up in terms of connectivity level and use. In addition, general engagement in activities on the Internet is high (75% in 2014). These data informs about the fact that there is a digital community with the necessary skills that is growing in the society. If services are put in place, these Internet users are supposed to be the first to become leaders in the uptake of digital services. Focusing on these strengths to complement investments on digital inclusion and multichannel service delivery, are crucial.

In contrast, in Hungary less than a half of the Internet users use e-Government and half of the individuals who use digital government services would be obtaining only information. These barriers are partly due to lack of knowledge about the service (30%) or availability (32 %).[9] These numbers show that there is a potential to increase the use of online public services by investing on back-office integration to develop more services and on a good communication strategy to better inform the service users. Communication strategies and techniques applied for the Danish e-Day (see Box 12) are good examples of initiatives supporting the introduction of mandatory policies.

General use of social networks (80% in 2014[10]) is particularly high which places Hungary among top EU Member States. In contrast, recent data shows that use of Digital Public Services is relatively low. Only about 31% of Internet users actively use "e-Government"[11] and Integration of Digital Technology to business processes appears to be among the lowest in the EU. The Strategy should address a broader policy context and include specific evidence as a background to planned actions. This can justify actions through creation of a context which is not limited to administrative aspects but of innovation. For instance, a proof of concept, analysis on why certain services solutions are selected, should be addressed.

Building grounds for business models and benefits realisation

There are numerous references to measures and indicators in the Strategy. At the customer side, a cost reduction of a -10% target for reducing administrative fee costs and a -20% target for administrative burden reduction are envisaged. Targets are ambitiously set and would require a presentation of a selected approach, impact assessment and business model. The background and justification behind these policy choices and target numbers remain unclear including whether realisation, risk management, cost-benefit analysis or other methodologies are applied.

Pillar three of the Recommendation on Digital Government Strategies underlines the importance of adopting cost and benefits analysis approaches (e.g. CBA, ROI), business case models and evaluation methods to secure a cost-efficient Strategy and allow assessment of various scenarios, options and react with agility to emerging circumstances. Among several countries Ireland, Germany, Norway, Estonia, the Czech Republic, Slovenia and the Netherlands perform regularly cost-benefit analyses for ICT investments.[12] Notably, the Dutch government reported for more than a decade that „all e-government–related interventions are systematically estimated using cost-benefit analysis"[13], while Austria bases its decisions on benchmarking and Australia[14] measures user take-up.

A trustworthy environment through better communicated and improved measurement and evaluation practices may be built and strengthened. It is remarkable that countries such as Denmark and Korea are those OECD countries which reported almost maximum realisation of financial benefits in their ICT investments[15]. Hungary is known for large-scale projects[16] similar to Denmark and the Czech Republic and this puts the country into a position where such approaches become valid concerns. It is to be noted here that the OECD Recommendation on Digital Government Strategies refers to pro-active and "structured approaches systematically" for risk management and "articulation of value proposition for all projects above a certain budget" and the Danish Council for ICT Projects determines risk factors "for any project that surpasses DKK 10 million (approximately EUR 2 million) and mandates enhanced project oversight where necessary".[17]

In this context it is worth to be mentioned that the OECD Recommendation on Digital Government Strategies emphasises the importance to develop clear business cases including "early sharing, testing and evaluation of prototypes with involvement of expected end-users to allow adjustment and successful scaling of projects." Both engagement and facilitation mechanisms with an intention to create a take-up level would need solid business cases.

Closing the information gap between ambitious targets and existing statistics

The Strategy sets targets and monitoring indicators and refers to a measurement framework to be set up. The current indicators presented in the Strategy refer to ambitious targets. It remains unclear if there are any baseline indicators and what is the differentiation between the targets such as +30% and +50% of case types available for electronic administration. There are insufficient details presented in the Strategy about which services have been selected and planned to be measured. However, such targets imply that there have been estimates and not all services are planned to be provided online.

There are key statistics already available and to be monitored such as the one provided by the Client Gate register[18]. As this solution provides a single point of access in the Government Portal to Digital Services: www.magyarorszag.hu, it could be a source for general statistics. This portal refers to a catalogue of services of partly or fully on 2,332 different[19] online accessible case types from which 400 kept up-to-date and around 139 cases can be started or even completed electronically. This is a rather high number and accessible to about 2.3 million registered users[20] by 2015. Based on this information it can be stated that about one-third of the Internet users have registration and therefore assumed to use online public services. Furthermore, based on Eurostat and OECD data from 2014[21] individuals who use the Internet to interact with public authorities mainly do so for obtaining information and only about half of the number of those actually fills out forms online. Facts on how many of the listed public services supplied by the Government are limited to information provision and which ones go further to a fully transactional status are not available.

In the online interaction between individuals and public authorities online, Hungary seems to perform below the OECD average and only businesses are an exception to this due to a specific policy on them such as client-oriented services and regulation. Process optimisation for digitalisation of services and benchmark on use by service types (e.g. tax, company registration) combined with smart feedback mechanisms could inform policymakers. (e.g. if certain services have a higher take-up, then analyse the reasons behind).

Recommendation: *Digitisation efforts and policymaking needs to be optimised based on strategic use of evidence.*

The Government explicitly recognises the importance of digital technologies as an enabler of a more efficient public administration. The Public Administration and Public Service Development Strategy 2014-2020 incorporates a vision for a "Digital State". The Government sets ambitious targets for a cost-efficient administration including a generous supply of services based on a "value for money approach" for all citizens. Nevertheless, there are several policy options to be explored which can support a more cost-efficient approach. As a matter of fact, the Hungarian society shows promising trends in general digital maturity which can provide a ground for higher take-up plans of digital government services. The following are some key actions that the Government could consider taking:

Boost competitiveness through more informed and evidenced-based decisions

- Analyse existing data and statistics to identify untapped potential and map users' digital capacity and digital readiness. Presumably, use and spread of certain technologies (e.g. number of smartphone users, Internet users and social media) indicates willingness and skills availability to use digital public services. Thus, broadening the knowledge and understanding of the existing digital environment in the country can serve as a basis for a more complex self-assessment and realistic objectives-setting.

Explore further uses of business case models to improve results

- The Government could develop, adopt and apply a business case methodology which better takes into account a broader set of criteria that sustain the selection of projects supporting a whole-of-government perspective. The aim would be to bridge the gaps between citizen and business interests on one side, and the Government's view in the choice of the digital solutions on the other. There is an overall need to provide details on how impact assessments, benchmarking, business models or other methodologies support the selection of policy directions and implementation.

Make more strategic use of data to prioritise digitalisation of public services

- Use the administrative portal (www.magyarorszag.hu) statistics more strategically, and collect and refer to data extracted from the multichannel services. Provide details on types and related priorities – such as which ones are fully transactional. Additionally, details could be provided on the plans for digital transition for specific services clarifying the expected timeline. The Government could consider including in the monitoring and evaluation process a mechanism referring to service types and benchmark their use as an input for optimal policy decisions.

Cutting red-tape by selecting key enablers and optimising decisions for going digital

Building on achievements in administrative simplification to go digital

Administrative simplification has been a core objective of the public sector modernisation in Hungary The ultimate goal of the Government is to improve both how public administration works and the quality of services towards the citizens. One of the outstanding achievements of the last years is the improved internal processes and development of e-Documents at all levels in processes of the public administration. This is reflected in the statistics as in the recent e-Government Benchmark[22] (2014) – Hungary's ranking on e-Documents (78%) is above the EU average (57%). This trend will be followed by the current Strategy and further links to the internal processes and services will be built.

All public institutions are obliged by law (the Government Decree No. 335/2005) to use electronic document management and it is mandatory to convert paper-based documents sent to the bodies to electronic ones. Nevertheless, e-Procurement could be considered as a next step for further developments.

The Simple State Strategy focused on reducing the burden on businesses and administrative deadlines, and case-handling time was reduced by nine days by 1st January 2014, resulting from combined actions such as legal procedural revision of Act CXL of 2004 on the General Rules of Public Administration Proceedings and Services and professional capacity-building in the civil service. The administrative reform has clarified taxonomies and created a harmonised system for the public administration. It is remarkable that the focus is on cutting red-tape and put key responsibility on the civil servants for better service delivery. This vision is confirmed by the fact that the „governmental offices" and multichannel (including digital) services have been created close to the citizens. Since 2007 at least 228 procedures have been reviewed. There is a tendency to categorise services according to certain criteria such as frequency of usage.

In summary, there is a strong objective to enable the optimal use of internal resources for improved service delivery and further targets by 2020 are indicated in the Strategy. Both administration time and administrative burden should decrease by 20%. In this context, how digital transition is planned to be implemented through the Public Administration and Public Service Development Operational Programme 2014-2020 (PADOP) and which services are selected to become fully transactional gradually should be briefly referred to in the Strategy.

One of the major factors that the OECD has highlighted in the early years of e-Government is the prioritisation. There should be a focus given to the "most common transactions for which there is a maximum potential for benefit to users and efficiency savings for government."[23] This leads to a conclusion that better targeted "fewer" services and priority given by evidence-based choice brings a higher value than aiming for having all services online at the same time. Consequently, modernisation needs to be accompanied with a strategic selection of those services which will be end-to-end online available. For instance, if internal processes and document management are electronic how e-Procurement could be built on the top of this.

Elimination of legal barriers from the digital way has been on the agenda and there is an explicit trend towards a next step to digitalise processes and manage the enquiries in a structured, co-ordinated manner in the back-offices. The legal environment allows fully digitalised internal operation of public administration as the Strategy states. Furthermore, users can have various market solutions for electronic documents and authenticate statements (e.g. smartphones).

Interoperability as a key focus area

One of the key focuses of the Strategy is interoperability. It is approached from the harmonisation of the databases/registers and semantics. Main legal barriers to reaching interoperability are reported to be wiped out and the Government is committed to create quality solutions for linking databases. Moreover, the Strategy sets an objective that 80% of registers and integrated services should be deployed by the end of the timeframe. This goal is nevertheless not accompanied with details on implementation e.g. the role of the National Telecommunication Backbone Network.

In this context, the case of Estonia where a real-time exchange platform, the X-road has been developed, can be an interesting solution to analyse. In Estonia the "once only" principle became a legal obligation in 1997 and the data exchange layer was set up in 2001. One of the success factors for Estonia was that there was political commitment to make this principle become a reality and also those real-time exchanges between organisations through X-road.

Box 4.1. Getting on the Estonian X-road – the governance process

Connecting an information system (no matter if government or private sector) to the Estonian X-road requires completing a process of metadata verification. The goal is to build a nationwide catalogue of systems (RIHA) and to ensure compliance of information systems with various requirements. Interested institutions can consult https://riha.eesti.ee to identify opportunities for automated data exchange. The national catalogue RIHA and the X-road system are maintained by the Estonian Information System Authority (RIA). Today, around 800 state information systems are catalogued in RIHA. All connected information systems have to go through a two-round approval process. The first round of approval results in the permission to establish a new system. The second round results in the permission to launch the system. Five state authorities are involved in the approval process, their supervisory powers are mandated by the Public Data Act and the process is fully supported by the RIHA web-based application:

- **RIA** checks compliance with fundamental interoperability requirements, e.g. the principle of non-duplication of data stored, use of the X-road layer. Information security requirements are also checked here. The interoperability requirements are defined in the Public Data Act and the Estonian Interoperability Framework;

- The **Estonian Data Protection Agency** checks compliance with requirements of personal data protection and data publication. These requirements are mandated by the Personal Data Protection Act and further exemplified by guidance documents issued by the Data Protection Agency;

- **Statistics Estonia** checks compliance with statistics production requirements, including the use of the National System of Classifications;

- The **Land Board** checks compliance with the National Address System and monitors performance as authority in all matters of spatial data (including EU INSPIRE spatial data requirements);

- The **National Archive** verifies that long-term archiving requirements are met.

Representatives from different institutions admitted that the process can be arduous and rigid at times. This is because the requirements by each of the five gateway agencies are not always clearly defined and partly overlapping. Nevertheless, it is generally accepted that this process has the benefit of identifying flaws in the design of information systems and their interfaces. Moreover, the benefits of having an information system catalogued in X-road are perceived as being high because this opens up opportunities for accessing policy-relevant

information in real-time and in formats that allow immediate use of that data to inform decisions. A recent event highlights the importance of the clearing process to ensure data quality used by the public administration and to reduce the risks of ex-post correction of initial design flaws. The Tallinn ticket sales database was designed to access and store a large range of personal data from national ID cards that can also be used for travelling. The data included a person's social security number, home address, e-mail address and other personal information and would be stored for seven years. During the process of X-road clearance of the systems these provisions were judged to be excessive and had to be corrected.
(www.aki.ee/sites/www.aki.ee/files/elfinder/article_files/Aastaraamat%202013%20t6lkesse_en.pd f)

Source: OECD information obtained from interviews in the Draft integrated public governance review of Finland and Estonia: Chapter on e-Governance and cross-border services.

Both solutions selected for ensuring interoperability and co-ordination among different organisations could be described in the Strategy. It is positive that the potential of interoperability is recognised by the Government as it is seen as a key success factor and a building block for digital developments which lead to several new opportunities.

Piloting electronic identification solutions and attracting users to trusted choices

User-focused delivery of e-Government when it comes to trust is often associated with personal data privacy and security that is collected and/or used in the process of electronic delivery. Hungary follows a rather cautious approach to privacy and security. The Strategy refers to the law on Information security and a complex approach which covers both intergovernmental and client security matters.

In Hungary the services are running on the central system and accessed through Client Gate which admittedly requires a new, secure authentication, and feasibility of several e-ID solutions have been tested (e.g.: student cards, public transport, card-based entry). The Government has launched a new e-ID card in January 2016. This card has modern features and solutions for identification. Future steps would be also to ensure use of the card, increase the opportunities for its use (e.g. services) and co-operation with service providers (e.g. Belgian e-ID card used and read broadly in services such as police, libraries, universities, banks, health insurances). Further details could be shared on methodology (e.g. functionalities or ROI, CBA) and how the e-ID solution is introduced, what are the targets for take-up and related business architecture.

This is in particular relevant in the light of the current user take-up on the administrative portal and how business continuity, communication is planned. If several solutions become a choice of the customer (as it is stated in legal ordinances) for authentication then the question is whether awareness is facilitated by the Government services and how standardisation among different solutions is ensured. The www.magyarorszag.hu is the administrative portal which serves as a single point of access when it comes to digital services and is known to provide access to all identified and registered users of digital public service.

The relationship between this new e-ID card and the administrative portal to access the services in a secure manner needs to be communicated to the broad public. Citizens need to be informed to ensure the uptake of the service by a sufficiently vast critical mass of users and the Government should consider specific measures to provide easy shift and clarity in rules and opportunities in order to ensure rapid take-up and keep the existing portal users satisfied over time. This implies a strategic approach to change management combined with a trusted solution by the users. In response to similar challenges the Estonian and Belgian governments have implemented effective e-ID solutions with a broad use and take-up level.

Box 4.2. Estonian e-ID solution

The **Digital Signatures Act** in 2000 recognises digital signatures as being fully equivalent to hand-written signatures, both in commercial transactions as well as transactions with the public sector. The Estonian national identification card and later the equivalent mobile-ID (jointly hereinafter: national digital ID) became the building block of a national personal key infrastructure (PKI), turning it into a legitimate means for authentication and authorisation in digital transactions, i.e. electronic signing. The dual use for commercial and public sector transactions, as well as the obligation for the public sector to recognise the national digital ID, created an environment that stimulated the development of compatible public services as well as their take-up by the general population. All digital public services can be accessed using the national digital ID, including electronic voting, electronic prescriptions, electronic health records, registration of businesses, declaration of residence, social benefits claims.

Source: OECD (2015), *OECD Public Governance Reviews: Estonia and Finland: Fostering Strategic Capacity across Governments and Digital Services across Borders*, OECD Public Governance Reviews, OECD Publishing, Paris. *http://dx.doi.org/10.1787/9789264229334-en*

Box 4.3. Belgian e-ID card

Belgium has created a mandatory ID card, which can be used for both governmental and non-governmental services. Public and private sector organisations have different access rights to meet privacy and security concerns. e-Signature and authentication function is included in the card and at the beginning of the project this was a voluntary solution if users wished to submit electronic forms containing sensitive data or financial information. The take-up was immediate. Legal background and piloting phase have ensured the success.

Source: OECD e-Government Studies: Belgium, ISBN 978-92-64-04786-0, OECD Publishing, Paris, p. 58.

Some of the experiences collected in other countries can feed an optimal decision while local needs are met. Co-operation between the central government and the local governments, closer to the citizens should also be ensured. Focus could be given to emerging solutions and business models for digital government services and other applications developed by private partners or users.

Recently it has been observed that in countries with a stable e-ID solution (e.g. Belgian e-ID card) several commercial solutions (e.g. libraries, schools) have emerged. Smartphone solutions are spreading in the business world (e.g. applications from banks). Tel Aviv, a city in Israel has issued an electronic resident's card (DigiTel solution, won a smart city award in 2014) in its own competence and built a smartphone application around it with different advantageous solutions from private sector providers (e.g. hotels, theatres, business solutions) which make it quite unique in its category. Linking initiatives among different players and stakeholders through similar solutions is seen more and more as a competitiveness factor in the digital economy.

Figure 4.1. Implementation level of key enablers in business vs citizen life events

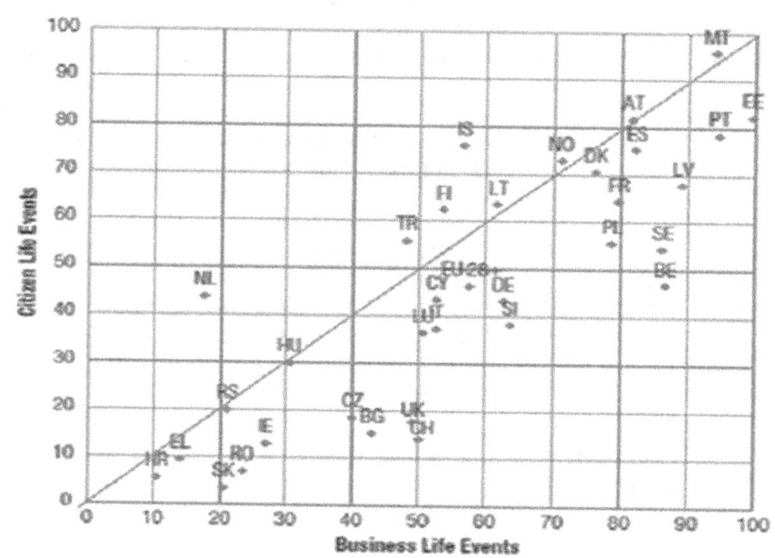

Source: European Commission (2014), Delivering the European Advantage? p.51.

Lead by example and promote a competitive environment in particular for a digital business environment

Hungary shows a balanced implementation approach on key enablers between business and citizens' life events (see Figure 7) but performs below the EU 28 average. In addition, only 16% of businesses use electronic information sharing technologies, and 5% cloud services while 8.9% use social media, among the lowest in the EU"[24]. Furthermore, SMEs selling online, Internet banking and online shopping is below the EU average. These statistics have an obvious impact on digital services take-up and in particular on areas which could create a competitive advantage for Hungarian businesses. The Government, based on the good example of having an open source competence centre which could promote other similar incentives for using cloud services and shared services. This – for both the public sector and enterprises – could be considered as a potential priority. This action can complement efforts planned to be made on service design and allow the selection of optimal, cost-efficient solutions.

Business continuity and a reliable platform for digital services

Hungary has a single entry solution for all digital public services (central and local governments) for customers (businesses and citizens) on the Government Portal, Magyarorszag.hu. This solution is easy to communicate and meets sufficiently the single point of access comfort for the users. Still, in 2013 the reasons for not using e-Government services in Hungary[25] was in 20% due to a „non-awareness of the existence of relevant websites/online services".

In the light of this we can conclude that awareness needs to be raised. On the other hand, over one-fifth of the Hungarian population is registered in the single authentication system (Client Gate). The concept of a single point of access for all users ensures an easy management of all existing stakeholders through www.magyarorszag.hu. On the other hand, there are several portals such as www.netenahivatal.hu; http://okmany.hu; www.kormanyablak.hu; www.kozbeszerzes.hu. These and other similar websites that contain public service (e.g. for companies, online documents, procurement)–related information should be linked to one single site in order to have a consistent policy towards the users, which builds trust in services and improves users' experience while searching for information.

Using data analysis and selecting policy options to promote take-up

The Strategy indicates several far-reaching objectives and indicators on the digital field which presumes that different policy options have been taken into account by the Government. The current references to targets such as 30% and 50% case types available for electronic administration would need to be complemented with information on take-up. The Government aims to conduct customer satisfaction surveys and reduce service fees. The business model behind these which could justify policy choices is vague and targets for the use of digital services is not included as criteria. Nevertheless, take-up is the main objective of any digital investment and should contribute to a better management of both human and financial resources.

Among the quantitative targets, take-up of the digital services could be included. It allows the "controlling" process to rely on the monitored take-up of services and to measure realisations, re-define interventions accordingly. In simplified terms when investments or service development is made, take-up targets by certain date could be defined. On the supply-side, digital services development must be a process that ensures the use and growing demand. Pro-active solutions, communication and channel management are certainly crucial aspects for a successful implementation. Furthermore, based on careful analysis, certain services can be offered mandatory on the digital channel similarly to how it is managed by the Danish government.

Box 4.4. Mandatory use of digital services in Denmark through pro-active channel management

The Danish eDay is an initiative where "the Danish public sectors on a specific date fulfil certain significant goals. Denmark has had four eDays since 2003:

eDay 1: 1 September 2003, all public sector organisations in 271 municipalities, in 14 counties and in central government had to send internal written communications by e-mail only, instead of by traditional physical mail.

eDay 2: By 1 February 2005, all citizens and businesses had the right to send secure electronic communication using the common public sector digital signature and encryption to public authorities and had the right to expect secure electronic communication from public authorities.

eDay 3: It had three goals to be achieved by 1 November 2010. Each public authority had to offer secure single sign-in using Nem-Login and the Danish second-generation digital signature NemID when accessing citizen-oriented online services. All citizen-oriented services had to be integrated into the Danish national citizens' portal borger.dk; all public authorities should have been ready to offer secure digital communication through Digital Post (a government-authorised digital letter box).

eDay 4: This marked the transition to digital-only communication between citizens and businesses, and public authorities using the government-provided digital letter box – Digital Post. The initiative is part of the Danish government's push towards mandatory "digital-by-default" – demanding citizens and businesses to use the digital channel only by law. eDay4 concluded a remarkable development of progressively introducing mandatory use of Digital Post for all. Businesses were obliged to use Digital Post by 1 November 2013 with citizens following on 1 November 2014."

Source: Information provided by the Danish Agency for Digitalisation in: OECD (2014) Spain: From administrative reform to continuous improvement, OECD Public Governance Reviews, OECD Publishing, Paris.

A strategy and action plan which set such an analysis into the centre and conclude on the most efficient solutions would create a strong credibility for the implementation.

Recommendation: *Cutting the red-tape by selecting key enablers and optimising decisions for going digital implies taking a number of integrated actions, from technical, legal and substantive perspectives. As many steps have been taken, there is a momentum to optimise both policy and budgetary decisions building on previous investments to deliver more visible results to the users.*

The Government has made crucial decisions on legal, technical and procedural matters. Investments on administrative simplification and electronic documents have created solid grounds for further developments. Hungary has created a legal option for interoperability and has set targets for co-operation among registers and databases. Some of the work has already been achieved and information lacks mainly on the implementation side. The actions suggested below are concrete steps the Government could consider taking:

Drive on past developments to take interoperability to the next level and deliver more visible results for users

- Build on achievements on procedural, legal and technical issues (e.g. information on reviewed services, created taxonomies and e-document practice) and create space for parallel testing and developments. Communicate efficiently the selected services to the users and scale them up gradually to become fully digital. For instance, there is a need for a clear implementation plan for interoperability clarifying different aspects (legal, technical, organisational and semantic solutions). Testing, which is ongoing for many services that will be available online in the course of 2016, was helpful to understand what needs to be further developed to satisfy broader reform needs. The enhancement of interoperability capabilities remains also a priority.

Maximise potential arising from the introduction of the new e-ID solution and consider complementary cloud services

- Select key enablers and analyse policy choices to support timely decisions on developments that are of highest priority (e.g. secure electronic ID and authentication when using a broad range of public and related private services). This should take into account the emergence and spread of new business models (e.g. cloud computing, smartphone applications) to complement the actions of the Government. This should include potential incentives that drive both administration and business to benefit more from both cloud and shared services.

Strengthen the one-stop-shop portal for online public services

- Keep on the good practice of providing a single point of access and consider business continuity and change management when introducing any new solution to ensure trust and better user experience.

Focus on targeted take-up of digital services

- Consider performing and presenting the definition of a vision and policy options on its implementation based on user take-up targets. Apply quantitative targets (e.g.

certain percentage of 1-Population, 2-Internet users, 3-Client Gate registered users to use by specific dates digital services). Consider mandatory policy as an option for those who are ready by adopting a "stick and carrot" strategy for certain digital services (e.g. businesses) and scaling them up while preventing digital exclusion. Clearly, the approach towards a "digital-by-default" service delivery, resting on a mandatory targeting of those users that can use digital tools should be introduced, while maintaining a careful approach that takes into account personal preferences. For example countries with important digital government advancements, such as Denmark, target user groups such as businesses or students.

Stronger governance and engagement as engines for public administration modernisation

Adequate leadership, governance and capacities for effective implementation

The OECD recommends[26] to governments to implement a digital government Strategy by ensuring "leadership and political commitment to the Strategy". This includes an "inter-ministerial co-ordination and collaboration, set priorities and facilitate engagement and co-ordination of relevant agencies across levels of government". In Hungary, there is a plan to implement a professional "controlling" mechanism to ensure better management of decisions and resources. A tendency to standardise these actions at all levels of the public administration is seen as a key aspect of effective resource management.

However, limited information is available on how particular aspects of the digital strategic co-ordination will be ensured. It seems that the Strategy lacks focus on the co-ordination mechanisms (e.g. including management of sectors and their strategies). Presumably it is the result of a specific situation that several measures are planned to be implemented through the EU Funds co-financed operational programmes. This puts the Hungarian administration into a position to follow certain EU regulations and meet those external requirements in the institutional setting.

One of the risks that has been identified in the SWOT analysis of the Strategy refers to a potential resistance to change and task allocation. This risk is not sufficiently addressed and there is limited information on the role of the different sectors and their institutions. In order to ensure that organisational needs drive the change with efficient co-operation among all stakeholders, solid internal governance and stakeholders' co-operation mechanisms need to be built. Combined with financial planning and support, prioritisation and strategic approach towards a digital shift would be a sufficient guarantee.

The OECD[27] recommendation on Digital Government Strategies refers to the importance of "clear business cases development to sustain the funding and focused implementation of digital technologies projects", reinforcement of institutional capacities and asset management. The Hungarian government has invested in improving internal processes and knowledge of civil servants to meet citizens' expectations. There are specific strategic documents complementing The Strategy with actions such as the Ereky Plan, the National Infocommunication Strategy and EU projects[28] which aim to build digital skills and capacity in the public sector. In addition, there is a need to ensure business continuity and a more predictable policy environment.

Capacity-building is an investment that can prepare the society to have more cost-efficient, digital service provision. Digital solutions allow re-allocation of capacities in a flexible framework. Hence, digital capacity-building needs to be measured and investments in customer support to be valued accordingly. The current multichannel service could provide access to users' demand and at the same time a space for transforming the relationship with service provision. A flexible framework of human resources and capacity management accompanied with user engagement are proven to be able to contribute to most efficient development and infrastructure systems. Re-defined collaboration frameworks and governance can support innovation and a more effective implementation.

Opening up processes and data for better value creation

Governance has an emerging aspect which comes with open government as an opportunity. Digital governments use technologies efficiently to engage better with stakeholders and create public value at lower costs than before. Openness, data sharing, development of content and services together through transparent processes can be a key factor for better performance. Several countries such as Malta, Estonia, Portugal, Austria and Lithuania which have comparable size and ecosystem to Hungary observed gains from closer relationship to citizens (see Figure 8).

The OECD recommends[29] Digital Strategies that embrace transparent, open and inclusive policies in their operations and processes. There are currently untapped potentials in early and constructive dialogues, digital engagement with the stakeholders. Openness, engagement, participatory processes enabled by digital technologies can improve take-up results in both the public sector itself and for users of public services. As an ultimate objective of the Strategy is building trust, this element deserves particular attention. Based on a recent report of the European Commission, Hungary performs below average in transparency indicators for service delivery, personal data and public organisations.

Figure 4.2. Transparency across life events 2012-2013 per country (%)

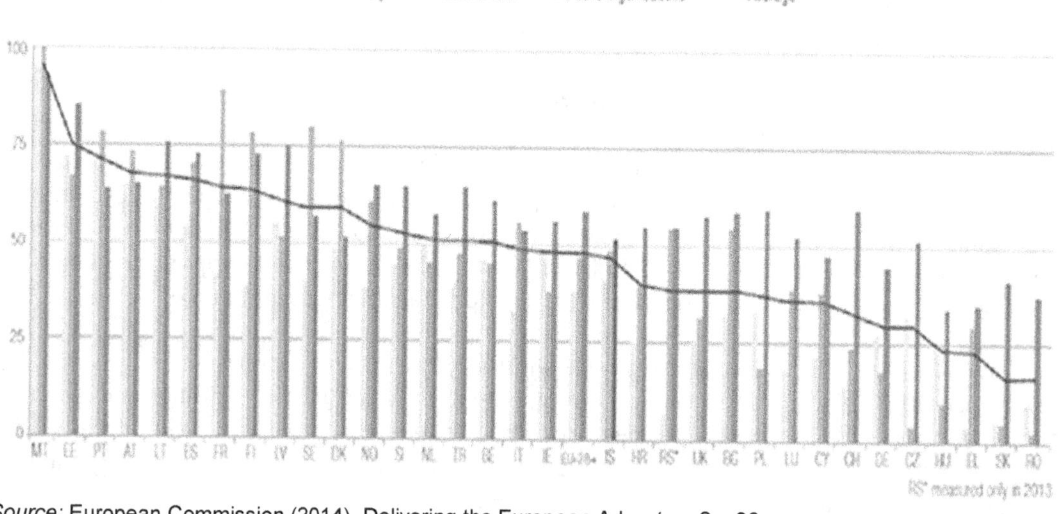

Source: European Commission (2014), Delivering the European Advantage? p.36.

Based on existing transparency statistics and perception of stakeholders more emphasis needs to be given to opening up decision-making and processes. Furthermore, service design and with the current technological support even delivery of certain solutions can become a shared responsibility. Open data is one of the tools where country experiences are available and can serve as a "food for thought" for the potential directions to be taken. Based on the OECD's findings[30] Open Data builds the next generation of civil servants and enable better value creation.

A creation of a "data-driven culture" in the public sector has been recommended to governments when focusing on digital solutions by the OECD[31]. This includes a development of frameworks for "guide, and use and re-use of the increasing amount of evidence, statistics and data concerning operations, processes and operations". It is seen that such an ecosystem that allows data supplementing and re-use by non-governmental actors or citizens can maximise economic and social value, which leads governments to introduce open data strategies. OECD countries engage more and more intensively in open data policy. About 22 countries have an open data strategy and 24 countries have dedicated portals.[32]

For instance, the United Kingdom since 2012 has an active open data policy that has brought obvious benefits. In addition, local governments such as London city have started to introduce their own data strategy. Local initiatives can support and test the introduction of a better open data policy (also as part of their smart city strategy) and advance efforts to foster open data re-use to create value and develop sound ways to measure impacts.

Box 4.5. Public Sector Transparency Board: Public Data Principles

The principles, drawn up by the Public Sector Transparency Board and revised as the result of consultation, are as follows:

(1) Public data policy and practice will be clearly driven by the public and businesses that want and use the data, including what data is released when and in what form

(2) Public data will be published in re-usable, machine-readable form

(3) Public data will be released under the same open licence which enables free re-use, including commercial re-use

(4) Public data will be available and easy to find through a single, easy-to-use, online access point (www.data.gov.uk)

(5) Public data will be published using open standards, and following relevant recommendations of the World Wide Web Consortium (W3C)

(6) Public data from different departments about the same subject will be published in the same, standard formats and with the same definitions

(7) Public data underlying the Government's own websites will be published in re-usable form

(8) Public data will be timely and fine-grained

(9) Release data quickly, and then work to make sure that it is available in open standard formats, including linked data forms

(10) Public data will be freely available to use in any lawful way

(11) Public data will be available without application or registration, and without requiring details of the user

(12) Public bodies should actively encourage the re-use of their public data

(13) Public bodies should maintain and publish inventories of their data holdings

(14) Public bodies should publish relevant metadata about their datasets and this should be available through a single online access point; and they should publish supporting descriptions of the format provenance and meaning of the data

Source: http://data.gov.uk/library/public-data-principles

Engaging with stakeholders and crowd-sourcing ideas from the digital government ecosystem

The OECD Recommendation of the Council on Digital Government Strategies[33] provides a definition of Digital Government, which strongly relates the use of digital technologies to the creation of public value. It also states that such a Strategy relies on "a digital government ecosystem comprised of government actors, non-governmental organisations, businesses, citizens' associations and individuals which supports the production of an access to data, services and content through interactions with the government." In this context, mapping relevant stakeholders and actors of the ecosystem (e.g. businesses, start-ups) and focusing on user engagement based on the principle of openness can lead to new opportunities.

Better engagement with relevant stakeholders and target groups of public services can lead to increased trust and efficiency. There have been concerns in the past about policy instability[34] and inefficient government bureaucracy and the Global Competitiveness Report of the World Economic Forum[35] is also identified as an obstacle for "doing business" in Hungary. The Government recognises the issue and commits to better communication to the public in good faith instead of immediate sanctions.

In the current changing policy environment (e.g. several new legal documents have changed) this communication approach can set the ground for building trust and promote behavioural change towards digital services in the society. The Strategy envisions the inclusion of users' views in the decision-making process and more pragmatic solutions instead of overregulation. An ambitious target is set for user inclusion as in 90% of the cases public service providers need to run customer satisfaction surveys and that no decision can be made without including customers' views. In parallel to this, the Government aims to decrease costs of services and fees for the users. This is quite an important and strategic objective as it has been observed[36] that governments' efficiency and effectiveness can improve by strengthening user focus and strategically engage with stakeholders. In line with this the OECD recommends[37] to governments greater "transparency, openness, inclusiveness of government processes and operations".

On the other hand, the Strategy lacks details on how to engage stakeholders, reach out to users and "build-in" their feedback into decision-making and implementation processes. The methods for user engagement vary in different governments and Hungary needs to take its own approach. Germany has set up user councils, Norway opted for communities of practice and the United Kingdom launched a portal.

The German government operates user councils at all levels of the government to optimise knowledge sharing, decisions and management.

Box 4.6. Germany's user councils for sharing information on infrastructure and services

In the area of services and infrastructure, the German government has set up user councils to support agencies of central and regional government. The councils offer a forum for members to voice their interests and consider the views of other agencies for providing "one-for-all services" (OfAs) and the basic infrastructure components – including an electronic payment platform, a central content management system (CMS) and electronic tendering via the Internet – that are necessary to deliver OfAs. User councils are involved in developing business models to ensure healthy development of the infrastructure systems."

Source: OECD (2005), e-Government for Better Government, http://dx.doi.org/10.1787/9789264018341-en *p.32.*

The Norwegian government in the last decade has built communities of practice to support developing human and structural capital and capturing relationship capital. They have estimated and reported direct savings with this solution.

Box 4.7. Supporting learning networks and communities of practice within the Norwegian public sector

The Norwegian government's efforts to modernise the public sector and increase the quality and user orientation of public services. The project builds on the idea that access to competencies and exchange of experiences are essential for local governments to make good decisions, become more innovative and produce high-quality public services. In order to achieve that, the project strengthens the importance of mobilising the intellectual capital of more than 700,000 employees working either for the central or local governments. This project's one of first objectives was to develop horizontal knowledge to support the development of user-oriented integrated electronic services.

Source: OECD (2005), e-Government Studies: Norway, http://dx.doi.org/10.1787/9789264010680-en, *p.99.*

The United Kingdom has "branded" e-Government services and managed the challenge or reconciling customers under hard budget constraints:

Box 4.8. United Kingdom government – Directgov (direct.uk.gov)

In 2003 the UK government launched a portal and shift from the agency providing services which "frustrates" users to a user-focused solution as follows:

- A clear and compelling value proposition to users that can be effectively marketed, without which the UK government will fail to attract the wide user base its departments need if they are to meet their targets.

- A capacity to manage service delivery on an integrated basis.

Clusters of governments' services and transactions targeted at specific user groups have been incrementally built and developed using "department store" and "franchise" models, allowing for structured, user-focused, manageable-sized packages of services.

Source: e-Government for Better Government, ISBN 92-64-01833-6; OECD 2005, OECD Publishing, Paris, p. 34.

In addition, the OECD recommends[38] to identify and engage with "non-governmental organisations, businesses or/and citizens to form a digital government ecosystem for the provision and use of digital services." New frameworks of collaboration could emerge on the initiative of the Government instead of isolated actions. One of the concerns is people who have the necessary skills and experience with other services but for some reasons do not use digital public services. Notably, if people are able to use certain private services similar to public ones digitally, there should be no reason not to motivate the digital shift gradually.

Building on the general use of social networks and social media, users can be reached better than ever on a cost-efficient set-up. More and more governments, also at the local level (e.g. Finland, Helsinki) tend to use social media as one of the many tools to "crowd-source" citizens' ideas and opinions. Moreover, similarly to the OECD, the European Commission has defined benefits of an open and collaborative government and encourages the use of cost-efficient open source tools to "crowd-source" or data-mining for better service design.[39]

Given the fact that in Hungary the take-up of social networks and social media by citizens is outstanding, the Government could consider fostering engagement through these platforms. A successful strategy can even appraise the impact of social media on customers' satisfaction with public services.

There are several cost-efficient, open source solutions that could be considered if open dialogues are performed regularly. Learning from other international examples could ensure that the Hungarian government chooses a tailor-made, informed solution. Good practices show how public institutions are increasingly reliant on online collaborative platforms. One such example is GitHub, an open source collaboration platform that holds re-usable source codes for www.data.gov (United States), www.gov.uk (United Kingdom), and many other projects.

Where governments fail to or are slow to use those platforms to improve and deliver public services, people and organisations step in and pressure for change. The impacts of "bottom-up" processes tend to increase where social media are combined with online petitions, mobile applications, open (government) data analytics, crowd-funding initiatives, and collective "offline" action such as protests."[40] These pressures for higher involvement are determining a shift towards more people-driven public sectors and public service delivery strategies.

Some countries such as Australia have a long tradition to build capacities and develop skills in the Public Service to manage digital government reforms; and the framework is being adapted to include social media and collaborative approaches"[41]. Several countries such as the Netherlands, Austria, France, Ireland, Canada and Turkey use social media strategically.

Fostering an engagement level allowing for new opportunities to co-design services

Most countries which perform better in user-centric life events intensively apply survey-based user orientation of services (e.g. Norway[42]) and engage users to design and define new web-based services. In Australia, Speechbubble[43] is an online engagement platform set up by the Government and citizens to co-design services. Several smart cities do co-creation of public services through digital participation (e.g. Manchester, Ghent, and Palermo). In terms of user engagement Malta, Korea, Germany, the United Kingdom and Italy (life events approach) provide international practices.[44]

Figure 4.3. **User-centric government across life events for citizen and business life events 2012-2013 (%)**

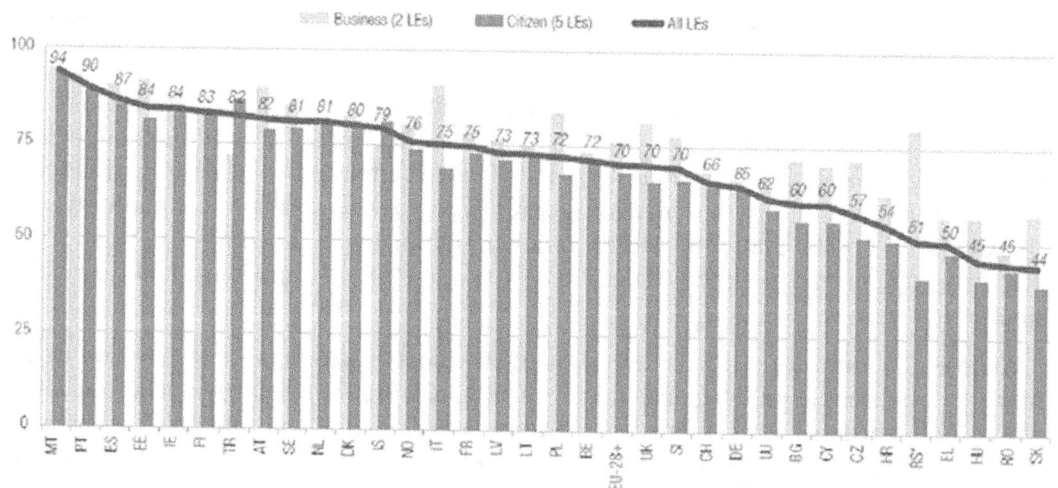

Source: European Commission (2014), *Delivering the European Advantage?*, p.27.

On the top of that, countries tend to shift attention from marketing and communication to a level of engagement to enable users to actually co-create their own services. This kind of co-creation for certain types of services can lead to cost savings and higher customer satisfaction. "Feedback from users can help refine service arrangements to make them more effective. For example user feedback on the design of forms or the way information is presented can help ensure that citizens are aware of entitlements and requirements."[45]

The Hungarian government could consider an engagement approach with a focus on user needs and feedback using modern tools (e.g. online collaborative platforms, social media, crowd-sourcing, and data-mining). This approach can include ambitious targets for "reaching out" to users and complement the public sector's internal efforts. If users with existing skills can be engaged, conscious public policy can drive them towards digital alternatives, which, in turn, can lead to cost-efficient and potentially innovative service design and delivery methods.

Recommendation: *There is a need to build up a governance framework with a view to supporting better co-ordination and stakeholders' engagement.*

Focus on strengthening governance and engagement engines is essential, as the reorganisation of institutional structures and governance frameworks can have an important impact on efficiency and effectiveness of implementation and results. Open data and new online collaborative platforms for stakeholders' engagement inspired by principles of openness and transparency can for instance produce strategic new business models to improve the offer of digital services and better meet different users' needs. The Government could consider taking the specific actions below:

Improve institutional co-ordination and collaboration processes and governance mechanisms

- Consider reviewing the existing governance framework for digital government to clarify the list of responsibilities and tasks allocation for all key actors among the different institutions. Establish the necessary dynamics and mechanisms to ensure efficient co-ordination in the definition and implementation of the digital government vision for the whole public administration. Describe in relevant documents, at forums and also on the web, the relevant institutional co-ordination processes and governance mechanisms in a way that enables any interested public organisation to notice its role and contribute to the Strategy's implementation. This should also lead to better co-ordinated, harmonised and more legitimate/accepted decisions which increase efficiency, sense of ownership and trust.

Contemplate open government as an option

- Elaborate on the aspect of openness and specifically on the opportunity for reform that open government brings to the administration. Consider developing a flexible governance framework that allows for strong co-ordination within the Government on "what must be done" (e.g. certain technical solutions) while at the same time bringing up a whole digital government ecosystem (including businesses, NGOs, citizens) to come up with solutions to "what needs to happen" (e.g. digital transition). Focus on developing a strategy towards open data policy to extend options for implementing new business models and fostering a "data-driven culture" within the public sector.

Plan stakeholders' engagement and benefit from closer co-operation through modern tools and   approaches

- The Government could consider including (1) a communication and strategic engagement plan (e.g. with targeted initiatives such as the Danish e-Day initiative), or (2) a social media strategy (e.g. UK, US), or (3) generating innovative service co-creation in partnership with different stakeholders (e.g. like in the UK). Additionally, evidence could be given on stakeholders' consultation and on how the Government is opening up during the policy-making process to support increased uptake of the new opportunities.

NOTES

[1] Public Administration and Public Service Development Strategy 2014-2020, hereinafter referred to as "Strategy".

[2] The Digital State is a core objective and measure described as „Development of enhanced electronic support" in the Strategy.

[3] OECD (2015a), *Hungary: Towards a Strategic State Approach*, OECD Public Governance Reviews, OECD Publishing. http://dx.doi.org/10.1787/9789264213555-en

[4] OECD Recommendation of the Council on Digital Government Strategies: http://www.oecd.org/gov/public-innovation/recommendation-on-digital-government-strategies.htm, p. 2.

[5] S.M.A.R.T.: Specific, measurable, assignable, realistic and time-related – Doran G.T. (1981) There is a S.M.A.R.T. way to write management's goals and objectives: Management Review (AMA FORUM) 70 11: 35-36.

[6] http://appsso.eurostat.ec.europa.eu/nui/show.do?dataset=isoc_ci_ifp_iu&lang=en

[7] http://appsso.eurostat.ec.europa.eu/nui/show.do?dataset=isoc_bde15b_h&lang=en

[8] All references are from the European Commission's recently developed index: http://ec.europa.eu/digital-agenda/en/digital-economy-and-society-index-desi, and Hungary: https://ec.europa.eu/digital-agenda/en/scoreboard/hungary

[9] OECD (2015a), *Hungary: Towards a Strategic State Approach*, OECD Public Governance Reviews, OECD Publishing. http://dx.doi.org/10.1787/9789264213555-en

[10] http://ec.europa.eu/digital-agenda/en/digital-economy-and-society-index-desi, and Hungary: https://ec.europa.eu/digital-agenda/en/scoreboard/hungary

[11] http://ec.europa.eu/digital-agenda/en/digital-economy-and-society-index-desi, and Hungary: https://ec.europa.eu/digital-agenda/en/scoreboard/hungary

[12] OECD (2015) *Government at a Glance* p.105. 5.6 Sectors in which CBA is usually performed

[13] OECD e-Government Studies: e-Government for Better Government, 2005, p.103.

[14] Further details on OECD countries' e-Government measurement are in "Rethinking e-Government Services: User-Centered Approaches", 2009.

[15] OECD (2015) *Government at a Glance*, p. 149. 10.4: Number of central government ICT projects with a total project value greater than USD 10 million. .

[16] OECD (2015) *Government at a Glance*, p. 149. 10.4: Number of central government ICT projects with a total project value greater than USD 10 million.

[17] OECD (2015) *Government at a Glance*, p. 149. p.149.

[18] The Hungarian Client Gate allows online access for registered users to access all digital public services. It has a secure authentication system and a single entry point to transactional services.

[19] https://ugyintezes.magyarorszag.hu/ugyek, the number of cases referred on the Government Portal.

[20] The Hungarian population is 9,908 million (2013); http://www.ksh.hu/docs/hun/eurostat_tablak/tabl/tps00001.html and based on the Communication from the Hungarian government on 6th November 2014 in response to OECD questions on digital government (on 1st May 2014, the number of registered Client Gate users was 1 700 627).

[21] GOVERNMENT AT A GLANCE 2015 (DRAFT VERSION FOR COUNTRY COMMENTS), pp. 160-161. 10.9. Individuals using the internet to interact with public authorities by type of activity (over the past 12 months), 2014 and 10. Businesses using the internet to interact with public authority by type of activity (over the past 12 months), 2013.

[22] file:///C:/Users/user/Downloads/HU%20(7).pdf

[23] OECD e-Government Studies: e-Government for Better Government, 2005, p. 33.

[24] All references are from the European Commission's recently developed index: http://cc.europa.eu/digital-agenda/en/digital-economy-and-society-index-desi, and Hungary: https://ec.europa.eu/digital-agenda/en/scoreboard/hungary

[25] OECD (2015) "Hungary. Towards a strategic state approach", p. 112.

[26] OECD Recommendation of the Council on Digital Government Strategies: http://www.oecd.org/gov/public-innovation/recommendation-on-digital-government-strategies.htm, p. 7.

[27] OECD Recommendation of the Council on Digital Government Strategies: http://www.oecd.org/gov/public-innovation/recommendation-on-digital-government-strategies.htm, p. 8.

[28] www.tudasodajovod.hu

[29] OECD Recommendation of the Council on Digital Government Strategies: http://www.oecd.org/gov/public-innovation/recommendation-on-digital-government-strategies.htm p.6

[30] Ubaldi, B. (2013), "Open Government Data: Towards Empirical Analysis of Open Government Data Initiatives", OECD Working Papers on Public Governance, No. 22, OECD Publishing, Paris. http://dx.doi.org/10.1787/5k46bj4f03s7-en

[31] OECD Recommendation of the Council on Digital Government Strategies: http://www.oecd.org/gov/public-innovation/recommendation-on-digital-government-strategies.htm, p. 7.

[32] OECD (2015) *Government at a Glance*, p.151. 10.7. Central/federal government support to Open Government Data

[33] OECD Recommendation of the Council on Digital Government Strategies: http://www.oecd.org/gov/public-innovation/recommendation-on-digital-government-strategies.htm

[34] Policy instability: This refers to the changing policy and legal environment from the users' point of view and not political.

[35] WEF Global Competitiveness Report 2014-2015: http://www.weforum.org/reports/global-competitiveness-report-2014-2015, p. 208.

[36] OECD e-Government Studies (2005): e-Government for Better Government, ISBN 978-92-64-04786-0,, p. 174.

[37] OECD Recommendation of the Council on Digital Government Strategies: http://www.oecd.org/gov/public-innovation/recommendation-on-digital-government-strategies.htm, p. 6.

[38] OECD Recommendation of the Council on Digital Government Strategies: http://www.oecd.org/gov/public-innovation/recommendation-on-digital-government-strategies.htm, p. 7.

[39] European Commission: A vision for public services, http://ec.europa.eu/digital-agenda/en/news/vision-public-services, pp. 6-7.

[40] Mickoleit, A. (2014), "Social Media Use by Governments: A Policy Primer to Discuss Trends, Identify Policy Opportunities and Guide Decision Makers", OECD Working Papers on Public Governance, No. 26, OECD Publishing, Paris. http://dx.doi.org/10.1787/5jxrcmghmk0s-en, p. 4.

[41] Mickoleit, A. (2014), "Social Media Use by Governments: A Policy Primer to Discuss Trends, Identify Policy Opportunities and Guide Decision Makers", OECD Working Papers on Public Governance, No. 26, OECD Publishing, Paris. http://dx.doi.org/10.1787/5jxrcmghmk0s-en, p. 5.

[42] OECD e-Government Studies: Norway, p.136. ISBN 92-64-01067

[43] http://speechbubble-blog.dhs.gov.au/

[44] OECD e-Government Studies: Rethinking e-Government Services: User-Centred Approaches, 2009.

[45] OECD e-Government Studies: The e-Government Imperative, ISBN 92-64-10117-9, 2003, p. 45.

REFERENCES

European Commission (2014), Delivering the European Advantage?, pp. 27; 36; 51.

"Getting on the Estonian X-road – the governance process" – OECD information obtained from interviews in the Draft integrated public governance review of Finland and Estonia: Chapter on e-Governance and cross-border services.

"Mandatory use of digital services in Denmark through pro-active channel management" – Information provided by the Danish Agency for Digitalisation in: OECD (2014) Spain: From administrative reform to continuous improvement, OECD Public Governance Reviews, OECD Publishing, Paris.

OECD (2005), e-Government for Better Government, ISBN 92-64-018333-6, OECD Publishing, Paris, pp. 32; 34.

OECD (2005), e-Government Studies: Norway, ISBN 92-64-01067, OECD Publishing, Paris, p. 99.

OECD (2008), e-Government Studies: Belgium, ISBN 978-92-64-04786-0, OECD Publishing, Paris, p. 58.

OECD (2015), OECD Public Governance Reviews: Estonia and Finland: Fostering Strategic Capacity across Governments and Digital Services across Borders, OECD Public Governance Reviews, OECD Publishing, Paris, http://dx.doi.org/10.1787/9789264229334-en.

"Public Sector Transparency Board: Public Data Principles": http://data.gov.uk/library/public-data-principles.

Chapter 5

Towards a budgetary reform in the context of the public administration and public service development strategy 2014-2020

The Hungarian public sector reforms have been weak on budget issues. In this chapter current budgeting practices and future plans of Hungary are discussed and an evaluation is provided on how far Hungary is from the move from line-item based budgeting to task-based budgeting, as well as the current status of performance budgeting and auditing. The link between evidence-based decision-making, the need to measure the results of the public sector reforms, the performance of organizations and organizational units and these budgeting practices are also considered.

Improving the quality of public finance management as a means to optimise the achievement of strategic national development objectives is a key challenge in Hungary, as it is in many countries. A feature of the fiscal consolidation agenda in a significant number of OECD member countries has been the re-design and reform of traditional budgetary frameworks, as part of a more comprehensive reform of the public sector and of public governance more broadly, and indeed as part of an economic restructuring agenda aimed at making their respective economies more competitive and responsive.

In many occasions reforms are undertaken in a partial manner giving rise to confusion and reform fatigue; moreover, crucial elements might be omitted threatening the achievement of the stated objectives. Whenever reforms are to have long-lasting and structural effects, it is important that the Government links the reform pieces together so that those who have to make it work understand how they are connected. So far neither the Magyary Programme nor the PAPSDS 2014-2020 has focused on budgeting practices. However, the new reform strategy 2014-2020 provides the Hungarian government with a unique opportunity to implement a comprehensive budget reform, which is, in turn, critical to enhance efficiency, boost competitiveness and contribute to the development of public administration in Hungary.

Linking the reforms to the budgetary process would increase their chances of success. The budget should be understood not only as a key strategic decision-making tool but also as one of the main policy documents from government. If the budget is comprehensive, covering all revenues and expenditures, the necessary trade-offs between policy options can be assessed against hard evidence as are the parameters of the Government's fiscal framework, allowing to optimise the use of public resources. Moreover, the budget supplies critical information that constitutes an essential condition for implementing strategic decisions rationally. Lacking a modern, responsive, transparent and outcome-focused budget process thus severely restricts a government's ability to perform and deliver strategic results to citizens and businesses in a rapidly changing environment. The OECD Principles on Budgetary Governance, as set out in the 2015 recommendations on budgetary governance are based upon the notion of inter-connected, mutually supportive elements of the overall budgetary framework and therefore could be considered as a valuable input to the Hungarian process of budgetary reform.

Linking the PAPSDS plan to the budget: the implementation of task-based budgeting

Historically, the link between the budget and the governmental plans for reform has been weak in Hungary. The OECD carried out a budget review of Hungary in 2007 already then it was stated that: the Hungarian budget has a strong and detailed input focus, at the time plans existed to shift towards a more output-oriented budgetary process (OECD, 2007).Furthermore, the review identified four shortcomings of the Hungarian budgetary process, namely a) the focus on the actual (non-cyclically) adjusted deficit, b) the focus on the budget year rather than on the medium term, c) the lack of rules for budgetary discipline, d) the lack of transparency concerning forecasts and outcomes. While Hungary has certainly made progress in many of these aspects, particularly driven by developments and requirements of the EU economic governance framework, several challenges lie ahead.

A traditional line-item budget, as the one currently existing in Hungary, is structured along the lines of organisational units and spending categories. As a result, parliament approves a long list of proposed spending separately as input items (e.g. labour costs, retirement expenses, grants to an agent, etc.) According to the results of the budget practices and procedures survey the Hungarian budget has 920 line items, and this figure has remained practically unchanged between 2007 and 2012, in stark contrast with countries such as the United Kingdom (40), Austria (74), Korea (90) and the Netherlands (122) which have a longer tradition in programme- or task-based budgeting. Furthermore, by its own nature the Hungarian budgetary process has been incremental, departing from the allocations of the previous year taken as a given and negotiating on the basis of increasing – or decreasing – those allocations.

The Hungarian government has stated as one of the objectives of the Magyary Programmes as well as the PAPSDS 2014-2020 programme the creation and implementation of a task-based budgeting system. It is considered that a task-based budget can enable the establishment of a link between strategy creation and budgetary planning. In essence, task-based budgeting groups several budgetary items under a specific task, allowing for the creation of a system of responsibilities as each task could be budgeted and evaluated independently. The core idea is that instead of budgeting for the organisation spending the money expenditures should be grouped and decided in terms of governmental objectives; therefore, all activities contributing to the same objective should be grouped under the same task, regardless of the organisational entity to which they are assigned.

The tasks in terms of which expenditure is classified and allocated in the budget represent, in general, groups of related outputs which share a common outcome – e.g. a preventative health programme, a primary school education programme, or a nature conservation programme. Importantly, these tasks are then broken into sub-tasks to give an even finer classification of expenditure by outcome. Expressed differently, the task classification of the budget provides the language in terms of which government expenditure priorities can be linked to budgetary resource allocations. In addition, tasks should allow measurement against pre-set goals.

Two main benefits might result from the implementation of task-based budgeting; first increased transparency of government spending and its results could be obtained. In addition, a clear link between tasks and policy objectives could be established. The integration of performance data into the budget would allow for a better accountability and oversight of government activities and priorities. Secondly, efficiency gains could also be obtained; these could result through two channels: allocative and operational savings. The former refers to the savings that could be generated from reducing the funding level of particular programmes while at the same time increasing the funding of tasks or programmes offering better performance. The latter results from changes in the funding level within a programme, as it identifies savings opportunities and/or fosters the attainment of higher efficiency levels. Streamlining government activities into tasks would allow identifying redundancies, which would permit the reallocation or elimination of tasks.

Hungary has made little progress in the implementation of task-based budgeting, stated as an objective in the current and past versions of the reform programmes. Nonetheless, the introduction of task-based budgeting is welcomed as a tool to improve public financial management and achieve efficiency gains. However, it would require important changes in the budgetary culture and major realignment of the budgetary process. At the baseline, it depends on the definition, type and amount of tasks to be considered and how they would fit into the broader structure of budgeting for organisational units and spending categories. The task inventory created under the Magyary Programmes could be a good starting point in that regard. Additionally, the implementation of task-based budgeting would require an agreement from the parliament to reduce its line-item input control of the budget in exchange for more information in outputs and outcomes.

International experiences related to the adoption of task-based budgeting vary widely. Countries such as the United Kingdom and France have strongly embraced task-based budgeting; others such as Germany have retained a classical line-item structure. Still others, like Poland see the co-existence of task-based budgeting and a line-item structure as a transition phase towards the full implementation of task-based budgeting.

Adopting task budgeting would certainly enrich government information on objectives and policies. In addition, it will increase the data on the effectiveness of tasks/programmes and the outcomes ensuing from them. Nonetheless, the budgetary process is usually subject to tight deadlines and faced with rigidities inherent to the budgetary dynamics; therefore, a big challenge would be how to incorporate the information as the basis for budgetary decisions rather than adding another layer of information to be merely used as an analytical tool.

In order to implement task-based budgeting, the Hungarian government is encouraged to set a clear timeline and action plan. Furthermore, all relevant stakeholders should be invited to analyse the scope and implications of adopting this budgeting system. An effective implementation should consider that tasks and sub-tasks must be results-based and indicators to measure its achievement should be designed. Moreover, tasks should be aligned with government-wide policy priorities. Tasks should be kept as simple as possible; many levels in the programme hierarchy could complicate allocation and measurement. Finally, the Ministry of Finance could create a special unit to provide support services to other ministries and agencies in establishing and aligning their tasks and common indicators. The selection of one representative set of tasks involving different spending units could be considered as a pilot experience that will serve as the starting point for the gradual implementation of task-based budgeting.

Recommendation: *Implementing task-based budgeting is welcomed as an efficient channel to modernise the budgetary process and achieve efficiency gains, and a clear timeline and comprehensive working plan should be set for the adoption of task-based budgeting.*

Making the most of task-based budgeting: performance budgeting and the audit function

Task-based budgeting is necessarily accompanied by the introduction of a performance framework into the budgetary process. Such a framework would allow assessing the results of each of the tasks as well as measuring the overall achievement of policies. Ideally performance information would be used beyond its power as an analytical tool and rather could become a decision rule for the allocation of resources.

While the use of performance budgeting varies greatly, almost all OECD countries now use non-financial performance targets/measures in their budgeting methodology. This usually involves government developing a framework through which objectives can be set and performance indicators can document results. In some countries objectives and indicators are developed as part of an overall strategic plan for the Government; in others objectives and indicators will be set and monitored according to priorities in a particular policy area. In practice this means a number of things. To start with information can be used to gain insight into how different programmes contribute to the achievement of the Government's policy goals. Depending on the type of performance information, this can also help explain why some tasks work and whether or not they represent value for money. Used in policy and budget formulation, this information can inform the design of better tasks.

Performance-based budgeting (hereinafter: "PBB") requires a collaborative, horizontal approach to be successful. Consequently, incentives should be in place for civil servants to work under a performance system. In addition, key skills regarding performance budgeting need to be provided through extensive training. These incentives could partly come in the form of positive recognition from the minister and senior management and partly through a greater transparency about implementing performance measurement as part of civil servants' annual performance evaluation that would affect pay and promotion.

The OECD calculates a composite indicator on the use of performance information at the central level of government. The index considers three set of components: a) the existence of performance information, b) the extent to which performance information is used in budgetary negotiations, c) the consequences of not achieving performance targets. The indicator ranges from 0 to 1, a score close to 1 represents a highly developed performance budgeting system. Hungary has a score of 0.25 which is below the OECD average (0.38). This result stems from the fact that Hungary does not have a standard performance budgeting framework in place; each ministry or agency is free to decide how to implement their own system. In consequence, all the responsibility to generate performance information as well as to conduct performance evaluations lies on the spending units. Moreover, performance evaluation is rarely or never used in budget negotiations and there are no consequences for not achieving the targets.

Figure 5.1.   Use of performance budgeting practices at the central level of government (2011)

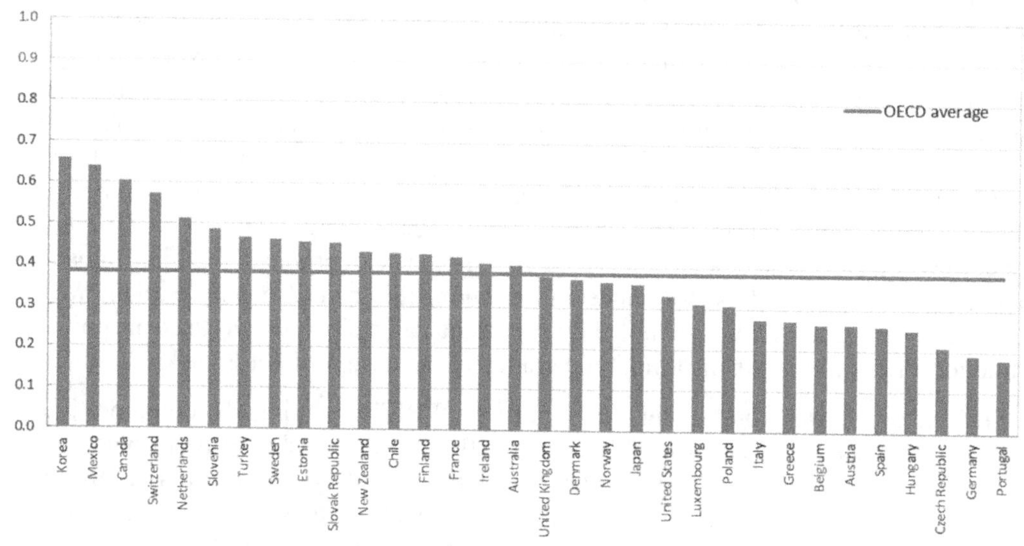

Source: OECD 2011 Survey on Performance Budgeting.

The process of adopting a performance budgeting system in Hungary requires the definition of a standardised performance framework applicable to all spending units. In addition, the framework should clearly stipulate a mechanism to assess if the objectives have been achieved. The experience of OECD member countries suggests that performance measurement works best if it builds on clear objectives, good-quality data and is embedded in a culture of constant learning and improvement. If indicators are not complemented with more in-depth qualitative analysis, or if they end up being imprecisely related to the policy objective or the programme, there is a risk that these indicators would lead to a situation in which rewards are given to programming that is not achieving its intended result, or is achieving perverse outcomes. Moreover, an exclusive focus on "what is measurable" leads to the discounting or non-measurement of other important performance objectives.

The ultimate goal of a PBB is to improve the allocation of public resources. If properly designed and implemented a PBB would enable the Government to assess whether spending is targeted to the achievement of its strategic outcomes. Furthermore, PBB strengthens allocative and operational efficiency, multi-year fiscal planning capacity, transparency and accountability. All in all, this would improve the public financial management system and should lead in the long term to the provision of better services to citizens.

Box 5.1. OECD Principles on Budgetary Governance

#8 Ensure that performance evaluation and value for money are integral to the budget process

a) helping parliament and citizens to understand not just what is being spent, but what is being bought on behalf of citizens – i.e. what public services are actually being delivered, to what standards of quality and with what levels of efficiency

b) routinely presenting performance information in a way which informs, and provides useful context for, the financial allocations in the budget report; noting that such information should clarify, and not obscure or impede accountability and oversight

---

> **Box 5.1. OECD Principles on Budgetary Governance** *(continued)*
>
> c) using performance information, therefore, which is (i) limited to a small number of relevant indicators for each policy programme or area; (ii) clear and easily understood; (iii) allows for tracking of results against targets and for comparison with international and other benchmarks; and (iv) makes clear the link with government-wide strategic objectives
>
> d) evaluating and reviewing expenditure programmes (including associated staffing resources as well as tax expenditures) in a manner that is objective, routine and regular, to inform resource allocation and re-prioritisation both within line ministries and across government as a whole;
>
> e) ensuring the availability of high-quality (i.e. relevant, consistent, comprehensive and comparable) performance and evaluation information to facilitate an evidence-based review;
>
> f) conducting routine and open ex-ante evaluations of all substantive new policy proposals to assess coherence with national priorities, clarity of objectives, and anticipated costs and benefits;
>
> g) taking stock, periodically, of overall expenditure (including tax expenditure) and reassessing its alignment with fiscal objectives and national priorities, taking account of the results of evaluations; noting that for such comprehensive review to be effective it must be responsive to practical needs of government as a whole.

More than half of OECD member countries have standard performance budgeting frameworks in place which apply to all central government line ministries and agencies. However, these frameworks are generally flexible and the extent to which the information is used varies for different countries. Based on the comparative results of the OECD 2007 and 2011 performance budgeting surveys, it has been found that performance information is decreasingly used for programme allocation and more commonly for management and accountability. Furthermore, the current trend suggests that performance information is commonly used by line ministries (e.g. different sectors) to increase spending and to a lesser extent to reduce or eliminate programmes.

Despite the current challenges to the use of PBB, the OECD believes that performance information has an important role in the definition of budgetary allocations. In the recently adopted principles (see Box 17) for budgetary governance, it is mentioned that performance information should be presented in a way that provides useful context for the financial allocations in the budget report. Moreover, drawing from the lessons with PBB in recent years, the Hungarian government could consider the following elements as crucial to incorporate performance information into the budgetary process.

Performance information should be accessible and oriented. The incorporation of performance information into the budgetary process would be instrumentalised through the generation of indicators, to be used throughout the budgetary cycle. In consequence, all line ministries and agencies are called to orient their processes towards measurement which could be reflected in the production of indicators. However, these indicators should be designed in such a way that they are measurable and clearly linked to the policy objectives. Furthermore, the number of indicators should also be restricted as an obsession with indicators can result in bureaucracy at the expense of service delivery. Moreover, performance information could also become a tool for managers and policymakers to hedge their bets and give veiled answers.

A key element to benefit from PBB is the existence of an evaluation system. Experience has shown that in order to use the budget as a tool for expenditure prioritisation a variety of evaluation elements and instruments are needed. These instruments should include ex-ante and ex-post mechanisms as well as the application of spending reviews on a regular basis. The different types of evaluations should have a clear "account holder" to determine the packaging of the resulting information as well as its appropriateness and timeliness for the budget process.

Performance information could become essential to strengthen the linkage between the budgetary process and the audit function. The supreme audit institution needs to be included as it is in close contact with the line ministries and parliament and needs to adopt and incorporate the performance framework in its standards. Currently, in Hungary, the audit function is limited to compliance-type audits; therefore, an enhanced auditing system could become an effective tool to promote good governance through the promotion of transparency and accountability in the use of public resources. Furthermore, countries such as Austria are incorporating the recommendations of the national audit institution directly into the budgetary process.

Box 5.2. Accountable budget: the Dutch reform

The Netherlands introduced performance budgeting in 1999-2002, this reform included moving from a traditional line-item budget to a programme budget where funds were authorised according to general policy objectives. The lessons learned from more than 10 years of performance budgeting resulted in 2012 in a reform called "Accountable Budgeting" (Verantwoord Begroten) although the idea was not that the fundamentals of performance-based budgeting were not working anymore. Instead, it was concluded that the framework of performance-based budgeting had created an overload of policy information in a non-focused way. In essence, after years of attempts to reduce the complexity of public policy in the budget documents, the Ministry of Finance was faced with the challenge of finding new ways to deal with this complexity in its programme budget. The core components of the reform are mentioned below.

Policy expenditures are presented in more detail following centrally detailed financial instruments. Accountable budget has guaranteed the existence of complete visibility of the major sums paid to specific organisations, agencies and institutions to fulfil specified policy goals, and in a broader context the role and responsibility of the minister for that policy field.

Organisational expenses (expenditures for personnel and material) are presented in a single non-policy programme, separated from policy expenditures. In principle this shift might appear to be against the principle of performance management according to which all costs associated with the delivery should be included. However, the effects might remain quite limited as most of the organisational expenses are incurred by government agencies and remain presented as policy expenses in the policy programme. Only the apparatus of each central line ministry is no longer divided between policy programmes. In this way all organisational expenses for policymaking and policy execution of a single ministry are displayed.

Policy information is limited to the information directly related to a minister's sphere of influence and the financial instruments used. Performance targets can only be included in the budget when certain conditions are met. If there is no direct relation to the ministerial responsibility and expenditure proposals, the information should not be presented in a budget document as an indicator for performance but should be used in other policy documents as an illustration of a situation rather than as a result of public intervention. In the Accountable budgeting framework, quantitative performance targets can only be included when a minister can credibly be held accountable for the results afterwards.

Focus on learning and referral to evaluation. A mandatory multi-annual table in each ministry's budget shows when each programme was or will be reviewed. This would guarantee that evaluations are not delayed. Second in the programme format of the budget, a reflection on policy adaptations and changes due to evaluation must be included.

Improved presentation of the flexible parts of a programme's budget. A uniform definition of committed expenses is now used by the ministries, resulting in a percentage of financial commitments in the fiscal year. For the percentage of the programme's budget that is still flexible, line ministries can explain which steps need to be taken to make the budget available for alternative allocation. One of the goals behind this reform is to limit the extensive possibilities that the previous PBB structure offered of using PBB for the purpose of policy legitimisation by line departments.

Source: De Jong, Marteen, Iris van Beek and Rense Posthumus (2013), "Introducing accountable budgeting: lessons from a decade of performance-based budgeting in the Netherlands", OECD Journal on Budgeting, Vol.12/3.

Recommendation: *The implementation of task-based budgeting should be accompanied by the introduction of the right performance budgeting framework. It should be designed in such a way that performance information could be used as a context for the financial allocations within the budget. The supreme audit institution should be integrated within the performance framework.*

Putting the pieces together: Improving cost accounting of existing delivery channels as the basis for the long term adoption of accrual budgeting

The PAPSDS 2014-2020 is oriented towards the development of a service-provider State. As a consequence, it grants crucial importance to the delivery of services; therefore, one of its main objectives has been the set-up of one-stop shops as a means of integrating services and achieving better delivery. The aggregation of services under a single provider presents a unique opportunity to generate information on the costs of providing different services. Refined costs could become a precious input in the process of implementing task-based budgeting as they would allow assessing the achievements of the different tasks. Furthermore, enhancing cost accounting provides a unique opportunity to progress in the direction of implementing an accrual budgeting system that should be considered a longer term objective of the Hungarian budgetary process.

An accrual budgeting system shifts budgeting from cash flows (money received or payments made) to revenues made and liabilities agreed. In other words, in an accrual system the limits to spending units are set on the incurred expenses rather than on the cash payments. Moreover, the term "accrual" refers to a fundamental accounting concept concerning the recognition of economic events in financial reports. Shifting towards an accrual budgeting system could enhance the effectiveness and efficiency of expenditure. By putting up-front the true costs of inputs and outputs accrual budgeting could boost both allocative and technical efficiency. For the former this works through promoting better choices about expenditures priorities, while for the latter it serves to inform the choice of inputs required to produce public services and enlightens the choice between outsourcing vis-à-vis internal production.

In principle 6 of the recently enacted OECD Principles on Budgetary Governance it has been recognised that budgets should present a comprehensive, accurate and reliable account of the public finances. Moreover, it is also stated that budget accounting should show the full financial costs and benefits of budget decisions, including the impact upon financial assets and liabilities. Accruals budgeting and reporting, which correspond broadly with private sector accounting norms, routinely show these costs and benefits; where traditional cash budgeting is used, supplementary information is needed.

The full realisation of the benefits associated with the adoption of accrual budgeting require to be embedded in a context of wider reforms; therefore, the PAPSDS 2014-2020 provides a unique framework to start moving in that direction. In the same line of task-based budgeting or performance budgeting systems reforms towards the adoption of accrual budgeting seek to keep managers responsible for outcomes and outputs while reducing control of inputs. In consequence, it is expected that managers should be responsible for all costs associated with the outcomes and/or outputs produced, not just the immediate cash outlays.

Providing further flexibility to managers to control their resources should be accompanied by the necessary information to do it. Accordingly, enhanced information on costs could set the stage for a discussion on the adoption of an accrual-based budgeting system as a longer-term objective. Moving towards accrual budgeting will imply defining, adopting, and implementing valuation methods and modifying the accounting standards. This process would require fundamental changes in budgeting and is only recommended when accompanied by a developed system of performance management and budgeting. Hence, the implementation of an accrual budgeting system should only be put in place once the necessary capacities to develop a PBB have been reached. Without these management capacities it is prudent for countries to continue upgrading their existing cash-based systems. Only countries such as the United Kingdom, Australia and New Zealand which are at the forefront of public management reforms have implemented a full accrual-based budgeting system. The diagram below shows the standard context in which accrual budgeting systems have been implemented and could be used as the sketch of a road map towards the adoption of accrual-based budgeting.

Figure 5.2. Standard context for developing accrual budgeting initiatives

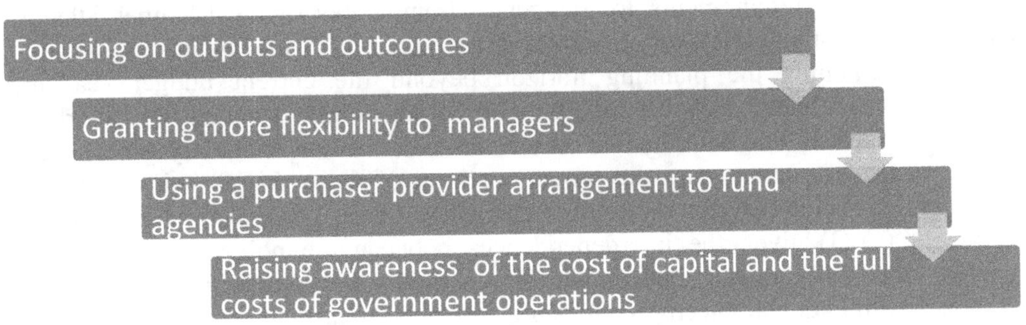

Recommendation: *The current changes in the service delivery scheme provide a window of opportunity to improve cost accounting; in turn, enhanced cost information could be used to nurture the performance system required in the context of task-based budgeting. However, in the long term, the objective should be the adoption of an accrual budgeting system.*

Framing the reform in such a way as to align the strategy with the constraints

Overall, the harmonisation between the policy strategy and the budget could be further strengthened in Hungary. A drawback of broad political programmes and statements is that they are not necessarily designed to align with the structure of the annual budget document; as has been the case with the PSPSDS 2014-2020.

In order to avoid the disconnection between the strategy and the budget the medium-term budgetary frameworks could be used as a channel to incorporate and internalise the dynamic effects of budgetary decisions. By strengthening the MTEF it could be guaranteed that budgetary trade-offs are considered and that a perspective beyond the budget year is taken into account.

A solid MTEF is a crucial element to help manage expenditures and ensure fiscal discipline. However, the impact of a medium-term perspective depends ultimately on the credibility of the expenditure estimates and ceilings, as well as on how this information is used by decision-makers and civil society. Failure to achieve medium-term budget objectives is often related to weak arrangements surrounding the preparation, legislation and implementation of budgetary targets.

According to the OECD experience, it is easier to link budget with the strategy if there is a medium-term planning framework. The OECD calculates an index on the extent to which a medium-term perspective is incorporated into the budget. Globally the index considers fourth components; the existence of an MTEF, the length, levels and substance of the ceilings, the quality and durability of the ceilings, and the monitoring of the MTEF. Furthermore, the composite analyses how often the ceilings are revised and whether or not it is possible to carry over unused funds. The results of the index show that despite preparing medium-term budget projections Hungary was one of the 4 OECD countries in 2012 that reported not having a Medium-Term Expenditure Framework (MTEF) in place as those projections are an informative element rather than a core guiding tool of budget negotiations.

Following the recommendations by the EU (Council Directive 2011/85/EU of 8 November 2011 on requirements for budgetary frameworks of the Member States) Hungary has recently undertaken a series of adjustments to its budgetary process, notably, strengthening the planning horizon beyond the current budget year to incorporate 3 years ahead. However, the binding nature of this extended framework is still to be assessed. In line with the OECD recommendations on budgetary governance and as a means of guaranteeing the proper working of their MTEF, it is crucial to nurture a close relation between the Central Budget Authority (CBA) and the Centre of Government (CoG) given the interdependences between the policy goals and the budgetary process. Moreover, budget allocations should be organised in a way that corresponds with national objectives and is aligned with the tasks.

Figure 5.3. Use of a medium-term perspective in the budget process (2012)

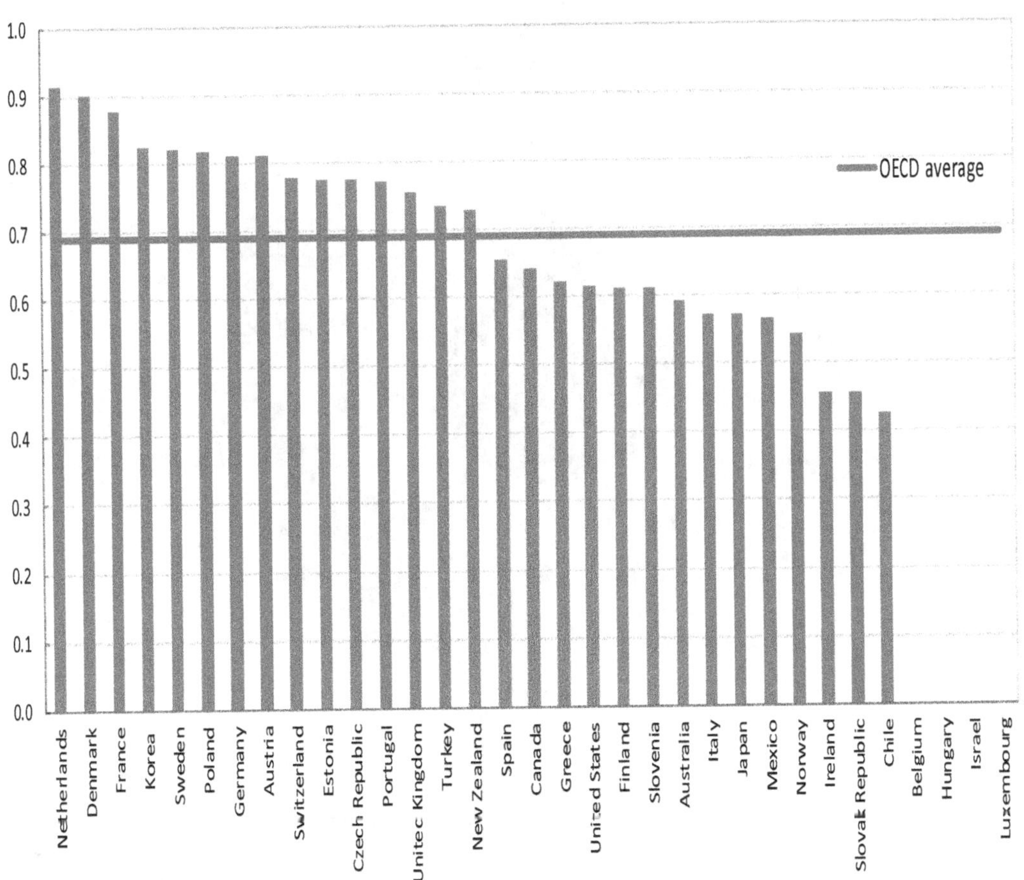

Source: OECD 2012 Survey on Budgeting Practices and Procedures.

Hungary has recently moved in the direction of incorporating a medium-term perspective into the budgetary process. In order to fully benefit from this planning tool the existence of solid political commitment towards fiscal sustainability is crucial. Moreover, in order to enhance the binding nature of the framework it is necessary to strengthen ex-post monitoring of compliance with the fiscal rules and be committed to the use of corrective mechanisms if necessary.

Figure 5.4. Elements required guaranteeing the effectiveness of a MTEF

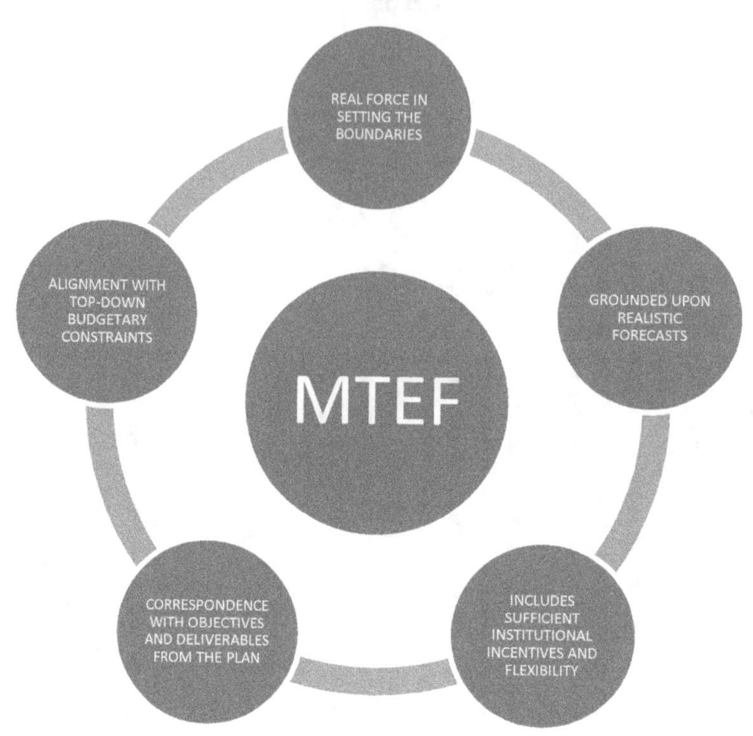

Source: OECD Principles on Budgetary Governance.

Box 5.3. The medium-term perspective of the German budget process

Similar to other euro-area countries Germany produces a stability programme which includes multi-year projections. For internal purposes the primary reference document is the Financial Plan. This document plays a crucial role in ensuring continuity of medium-term fiscal planning from one annual budget cycle to the next. This plan contains projections for a five-year-period, the current year, the upcoming budget year and the following three years. The financial plan is presented for information purposes and is not formally approved by the parliament, moreover it is not considered binding in any sense upon the budgetary processes and decisions. However, once a final version of the financial plan is laid down and approved by government it comprises commitments and decisions allowing limited room for discretion or ambiguity. In practical terms, it assumes significant influence over the shape of budgetary policy and guides budgetary policy unless some external shock occurs.

Source: OECD (2014) Budget Review Germany.

Recommendation: *There is a need to harmonise policy strategies and the budget decisions by guaranteeing the binding nature of the medium-term budgetary framework.*

REFERENCES

De Jong, Marteen, Iris van Beek and Rense Posthumus (2013), "Introducing accountable budgeting: lessons from a decade of performance-based budgeting in the Netherlands", OECD Journal on Budgeting, Vol.12/3.

OECD (2011), Survey on Performance Budgeting.

OECD (2012), Survey on Budgeting Practices and Procedures.

OECD (2014), Budget Review Germany.

OECD (2015), OECD Principles on Budgetary Governance.

OECD (2013), Government at a Glance 2013 edition, OECD Publishing, Paris.

ORGANISATION FOR ECONOMIC CO-OPERATION AND DEVELOPMENT

The OECD is a unique forum where governments work together to address the economic, social and environmental challenges of globalisation. The OECD is also at the forefront of efforts to understand and to help governments respond to new developments and concerns, such as corporate governance, the information economy and the challenges of an ageing population. The Organisation provides a setting where governments can compare policy experiences, seek answers to common problems, identify good practice and work to co-ordinate domestic and international policies.

The OECD member countries are: Australia, Austria, Belgium, Canada, Chile, the Czech Republic, Denmark, Estonia, Finland, France, Germany, Greece, Hungary, Iceland, Ireland, Israel, Italy, Japan, Korea, Latvia, Luxembourg, Mexico, the Netherlands, New Zealand, Norway, Poland, Portugal, the Slovak Republic, Slovenia, Spain, Sweden, Switzerland, Turkey, the United Kingdom and the United States. The European Union takes part in the work of the OECD.

OECD Publishing disseminates widely the results of the Organisation's statistics gathering and research on economic, social and environmental issues, as well as the conventions, guidelines and standards agreed by its members.

OECD PUBLISHING, 2, rue André-Pascal, 75775 PARIS CEDEX 16
(42 2017 50 1 P) ISBN 978-92-64-28398-5 – 2017